BOOK 2

STEP-BY-STEP
WRITING

A STANDARDS-BASED APPROACH

Linda Lonon Blanton

THOMSON
—✳—
HEINLE

Australia • Canada • Mexico • Singapore • United Kingdom • United States

STEP–BY–STEP WRITING, Book 2
Linda Lonon Blanton

Publisher, School ESL: *Sherrise Roehr*
VP, Director of Content Development: *Anita Raducanu*
Development Editor: *Margarita Matte*
Associate Development Editor: *Catherine McCue*
Director of Product Marketing: *Amy Mabley*
Executive Marketing Manager: *Jim McDonough*
Associate Content Project Manager: *John Sarantakis*

Frontlist Buyer: *Susan Carroll*
Contributing Writer: *Susan Jones Leeming*
Project Manager: *Tunde Dewey*
Composition: *Pre-Press PMG*
Cover Design: *Sibler Design*
Printer: *Transcontinental*

Printed in Canada.
1 2 3 4 5 6 7 8 9 10 — 11 10 09 08 07

For more information contact Thomson Heinle, 25 Thomson Place, Boston, Massachusetts 02210 USA, or you can visit our Internet site at http://elt.thomson.com

Dictionary definitions from *Heinle's Newbury House Dictionary.*

For permission to use material from this text or product, submit a request online at http://www.thomsonrights.com

Any additional questions about permissions can be submitted by email to thomsonrights@thomson.com

ISBN: 978-1-4240-0401-0
ISE ISBN: 978-1-4240-0504-8

Library of Congress Control Number: 2007932076

ACKNOWLEDGMENTS

Thomson Heinle would like to thank the following consultants and reviewers:

Consultants

Jennifer Runner
Atwater High School
Atwater, California

Patricia Levine
Colts Neck High School
Colts Neck, New Jersey

Alicia Bartol-Thomas
Sarasota County Schools
Sarasota, Florida

Vivian K. Kahn
Halsey Intermediate School 296
New York City Dept. of Education
Brooklyn, New York

Reviewers

Teresa Arvizu
McFarland Unified School District
McFarland, California

M. Danielle Bragaw
Bedichek Middle School
Austin, Texas

Gary Bechtold
New Boston Pilot Middle School
Dorchester, Massachusetts

Maria Celis
Lamar High School
Houston, Texas

Linda Contreras
Luther Burbank High School
Sacramento, California

Susannah Courand
T.C. Williams High School
Alexandria, Virginia

Dana Dusbiber
Luther Burbank High School
Sacramento, California

Sara Farley
Wichita High School East
Wichita, Kansas

Sharolyn Hutton
Newcomer School
Ontario, California

Barbara Ishida
Downey High School
Modesto, California

Dana Liebowitz
Palm Beach Central High School
Wellington, Florida

Barbara M. Linde
YorkTown, Virginia

Andrew Lukov
School District of Philadelphia
Philadelphia, Pennsylvania

Jennifer Olsen
Chiefess Kamakahelei Middle
  School
Lihue, Hawaii

Mary Susan Osborn-Iratene
Will Rogers Middle School
Fair Oaks, California

Diana Sefchik
North Plainfield High School
North Plainfield, New Jersey

Malgorzata Stone
Franklin High School
Seattle, Washington

Alison Tepper
Western Middle School
Greenwich, Connecticut

Mark Trzasko
Okeeheelee Middle School
West Palm Beach, Florida

Karin VonRiman
Abraham Clark High School
Roselle, New Jersey

Deborah Wilkes
Lee County High School
Sanford, North Carolina

Clara Wolfe
William Allen High School
Allentown, Pennsylvania

TABLE OF CONTENTS

How to use this book

Discuss
Talk about the pictures.

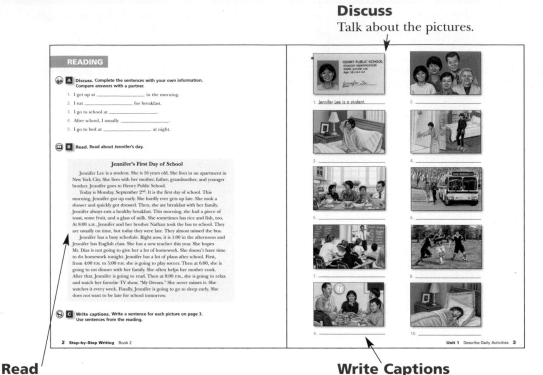

Read
Read a short passage. This models new language you can use for your writing.

Write Captions
Write captions to describe the pictures. This helps to understand how to use new words and sentences.

Vocabulary
Practice the words you need.

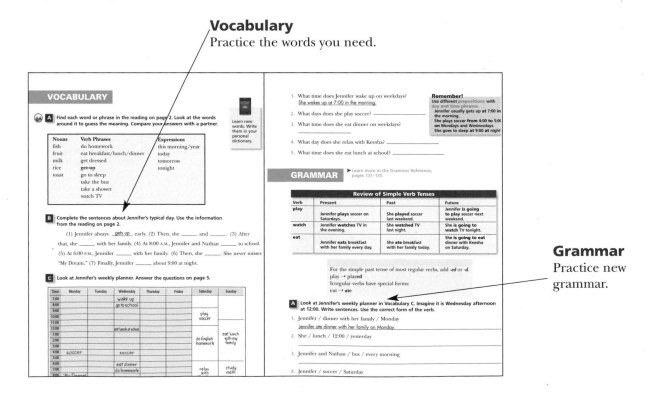

Grammar
Practice new grammar.

Remember!
Learn language points and ways to improve your writing.

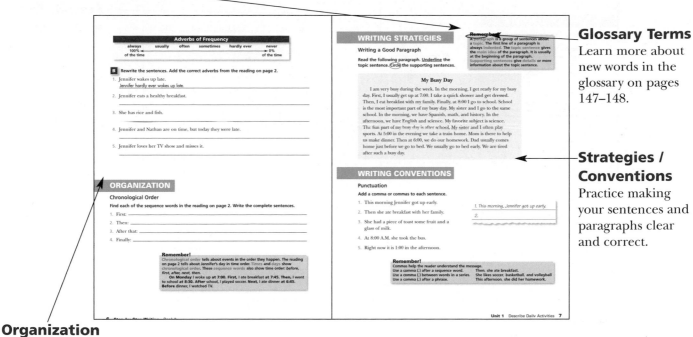

WRITING STRATEGIES
Writing a Good Paragraph

Read the following paragraph. Underline the topic sentence. Circle the supporting sentences.

Remember!
A paragraph is a group of sentences about a topic. The first line of a paragraph is always indented. The topic sentence gives the main idea of the paragraph. It is usually at the beginning of the paragraph. Supporting sentences give details or more information about the topic sentence.

My Busy Day

I am very busy during the week. In the morning, I get ready for my busy day. First, I usually get up at 7:00. I take a quick shower and get dressed. Then, I eat breakfast with my family. Finally, at 8:00 I go to school. School is the most important part of my busy day. My sister and I go to the same school. In the morning, we have Spanish, math, and history. In the afternoon, we have English and science. My favorite subject is science. The fun part of my busy day is after school. My sister and I often play sports. At 5:00 in the evening we take a train home. Mom is there to help us make dinner. Then at 6:00, we do our homework. Dad usually comes home just before we go to bed. We usually go to bed early. We are tired after such a busy day.

WRITING CONVENTIONS
Punctuation

Add a comma or commas to each sentence.

1. This morning Jennifer got up early.
2. Then she ate breakfast with her family.
3. She had a piece of toast some fruit and a glass of milk.
4. At 8:00 A.M. she took the bus.
5. Right now it is 1:00 in the afternoon.

1. This morning, Jennifer got up early.
2.

Remember!
Commas help the reader understand the message.
Use a comma (,) after a sequence word.   Then, she ate breakfast.
Use a comma (,) between words in a series.   She likes soccer, basketball, and volleyball.
Use a comma (,) after a phrase.   This afternoon, she did her homework.

Adverbs of Frequency

always	usually	often	sometimes	hardly ever	never
100%					0%
of the time					of the time

B Rewrite the sentences. Add the correct adverbs from the reading on page 2.

1. Jennifer wakes up late.
   Jennifer hardly ever wakes up late.

2. Jennifer eats a healthy breakfast.

3. She has rice and fish.

4. Jennifer and Nathan are on time, but today they were late.

5. Jennifer loves her TV show and misses it.

ORGANIZATION
Chronological Order

Find each of the sequence words in the reading on page 2. Write the complete sentences.

1. First:
2. Then:
3. After that:
4. Finally:

Remember!
Chronological order tells about events in the order they happen. The reading on page 2 tells about Jennifer's day in time order. Times and days show chronological order. These sequence words also show time order: before, first, after, next, then.
On Monday I woke up at 7:00. First, I ate breakfast at 7:45. Then, I went to school at 8:30. After school, I played soccer. Next, I ate dinner at 6:45. Before dinner, I watched TV.

Step-by-Step Writing · Book 2

Unit 1 Describe Daily Activities **7**

Glossary Terms
Learn more about new words in the glossary on pages 147–148.

Strategies / Conventions
Practice making your sentences and paragraphs clear and correct.

Organization
Practice ways to organize information.

Writing
See a model of a student's writing. This helps you understand your goal.

WRITING
Narrative Writing

Narration tells a story. It can describe a series of events or tell about one specific event. In narration paragraphs, the topic sentence introduces the story. The supporting sentences tell what happens in the story. The concluding sentence ends the story, summarizes the story, or tells why it is important. Journal entries and personal essays are examples of narrations.

A Read. Read Caleb's journal entry.

Learn new words. Write them in your personal dictionary.

My Busy Weekends

My weekends are usually really busy, but they are fun. Everyone in my family has different activities each weekend. We usually wake up early and eat breakfast at home. Sometimes we have a game or class in the afternoon. On Sunday, we always have a big dinner with my grandfather. Last Saturday was very busy. We went to my football game from 10:00 to 12:00. After the game we ate lunch at our favorite restaurant. At 2:00, my brother and I went to our music lessons. I play the piano. My brother plays the violin. Then in the evening, we had a picnic in the park from 6:00 to 7:30. Next weekend is going to be very exciting. On Saturday, we are going to drive to Boston. We are going to go to a big party for my grandmother. She is going to be sixty years old. After the party, we are going to stay at my cousin's house. Next weekend is going to be busy, but it is going to be special.

Caleb's Weekend Activities

| 02.01.13 TK | 02.01.14 TK | 02.01.15 TK |

Usual Weekend Activities	Last Weekend's Activities	Next Weekend's Activities
1. Caleb and his family usually wake up early and eat breakfast at home.	4.	8.
2.	5.	9.
	6.	
3.	7.	10.

Caleb's weekends are usually really busy, but fun. Caleb and his family usually wake up early and eat breakfast at home. Sometimes they . . . .

(continued on the following page)

Writing Prompt
Read the writing prompt.
This tells you what to do.

Step 1: Pre-write
Look at model notes and a graphic organizer.
Then you think of ideas and take notes.

Step 3: Draft and Revise
Look at a model first draft and make corrections. Then you write your own first draft. You think of how to improve your writing. Then you revise your writing.

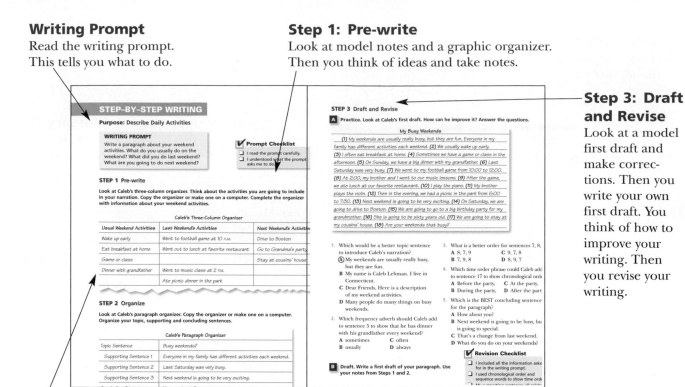

Step 2: Organize
You put your ideas in order. This will help the reader to understand your writing.

Step 4: Edit
Find errors in model sentences and correct them. Then, you edit your own draft. In Peer Edit, exchange drafts with a partner. Then make suggestions for improvement.

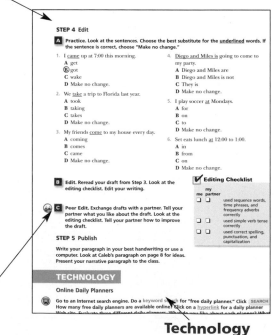

Step 5: Publish
Make a final draft of your writing. Now you can share it with your class or your family.

Technology
Use a computer to find and format new information.

Why is writing important?

With good writing skills, you can:

 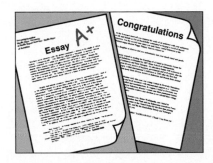 

Connect	Succeed	Express
- connect with people	- do better in school	- describe and explain your experiences
	- get a job or get into college	
- write letters, e-mail, instructions, speeches, posters, articles, descriptions, and summaries	- write essays, book reports, applications, and persuasive business letters	- write journal entries, descriptions, stories, and poems

What are good writing habits?

Good writers think about . . .	Questions	Examples
Form	What does the writing look like?	a letter, a paragraph, a list
Audience	Who will read my writing?	a friend, a teacher, someone I don't know
Topic	What is the writing about?	my weekend, my school, a celebration
Purpose	Why am I writing?	to describe, to inform, to persuade

What are the types of writing?

Are you writing to describe someone? Are you writing to tell how something looks, tastes, feels, smells, sounds? This is called **descriptive writing.**

Are you writing to tell about something that happened? This is called **narrative writing.**

Are you writing to explain facts to the reader? This is called **expository writing.**

Do you want the reader to do something? This is called **persuasive writing.**

Are you writing to explain a process or procedure? This is called **technical writing.**

Are you writing a message to someone? This is called **letter writing.**

Are you writing about something you read? This is called a **response to literature.**

Unit 1

Describe Daily Activities

UNIT OBJECTIVES

Writing
narrative writing

Organization
chronological order

Writing Strategies
writing a good paragraph

Writing Conventions
punctuation

Vocabulary
daily activities
time expressions

Grammar
review of simple verb tenses
adverbs of frequency

Technology
researching online daily planners

HENRY PUBLIC SCHOOL
STUDENT IDENTIFICATION
NAME: Jennifer Lee
Age: 16 years old

Jennifer Lee
Signature

Caleb's Weekend Activities

Usual Weekend Activities	Last Weekend's Activities	Next Weekend's Activities
1. Caleb and his family usually wake up early and eat breakfast at home.	4.	8.
2.	5.	9.
3.	6.	10.
	7.	

Caleb's weekends are usually really busy, but fun. Caleb and his family usually wake up early and eat breakfast at home. Sometimes they . . . .

A Discuss. Complete the sentences with your own information. Compare answers with a partner.

1. I get up at _____ in the morning.

2. I eat _____ for breakfast.

3. I go to school at _____.

4. After school, I usually _____.

5. I go to bed at _____ at night.

B Read. Read about Jennifer's day.

Jennifer's First Day of School

Jennifer Lee is a student. She is sixteen years old. She lives in an apartment in New York City. She lives with her mother, father, grandmother, and younger brother. Jennifer goes to Henry Public School.

Today is Monday, September 2nd. It is the first day of school. This morning, Jennifer got up early. She hardly ever gets up late. She took a shower and quickly got dressed. Then, she ate breakfast with her family. Jennifer always eats a healthy breakfast. This morning, she had a piece of toast, some fruit, and a glass of milk. She sometimes has rice and fish, too. At 8:00 A.M., Jennifer and her brother Nathan took the bus to school. They are usually on time, but today they were late. They almost missed the bus.

Jennifer has a busy schedule. Right now, it is 1:00 in the afternoon and Jennifer has English class. She has a new teacher this year. She hopes Mr. Diaz is not going to give her a lot of homework. She doesn't have time to do homework tonight. Jennifer has a lot of plans after school. First, from 4:00 P.M. to 5:00 P.M. she is going to play soccer. Then at 6:00, she is going to eat dinner with her family. She often helps her mother cook. After that, Jennifer is going to read. Then at 8:00 P.M., she is going to relax and watch her favorite TV show, "My Dream." She never misses it. She watches it every week. Finally, Jennifer is going to go to sleep early. She does not want to be late for school tomorrow.

 C Write captions. Write a sentence for each picture on page 3. Use sentences from the reading.

1. <u>Jennifer Lee is a student.</u> _____

2. _____

3. _____

4. _____

5. _____

6. _____

7. _____

8. _____

9. _____

10. _____

VOCABULARY

 A Find each word or phrase in the reading on page 2. Look at the words around it to guess the meaning. Compare your answers with a partner.

Learn new words. Write them in your personal dictionary.

Nouns	Verb Phrases	Expressions
fish	do homework	this morning/year
fruit	eat breakfast/lunch/dinner	today
milk	get dressed	tomorrow
rice	get up	tonight
toast	go to sleep	
	take the bus	
	take a shower	
	watch TV	

B Complete the sentences about Jennifer's typical day. Use the information from the reading on page 2.

(1) Jennifer always ___gets up___ early. (2) Then, she _____ and _____. (3) After that, she _____ with her family. (4) At 8:00 A.M., Jennifer and Nathan _____ to school. (5) At 6:00 P.M., Jennifer _____ with her family. (6) Then, she _____. She never misses "My Dream." (7) Finally, Jennifer _____ about 9:00 at night.

C Look at Jennifer's weekly planner. Answer the questions on page 5.

Time	Monday	Tuesday	Wednesday	Thursday	Friday	Saturday	Sunday
7:00	wake up						
8:00	go to school						
9:00						play soccer	
10:00							
11:00							
12:00	eat lunch at school						
1:00							eat lunch with my family
2:00						do English homework	
3:00							
4:00	soccer		soccer				
5:00							
6:00	eat dinner						
7:00	do homework					relax with Keesha	study math
8:00	"My Dream"						
9:00	sleep early						sleep
10:00						sleep	

1. What time does Jennifer wake up on weekdays?
   <u>She wakes up at 7:00 in the morning.</u>

2. What days does she play soccer? _____

3. What time does she eat dinner on weekdays?
   _____

4. What day does she relax with Keesha? _____

5. What time does she eat lunch at school? _____

►Learn more in the Grammar Reference, pages 149–164.

GRAMMAR

Review of Simple Verb Tenses

Verb	Present	Past	Future
play	Jennifer **plays** soccer on Saturdays.	She **played** soccer last weekend.	Jennifer **is going to play** soccer next weekend.
watch	Jennifer **watches** TV in the evening.	She **watched** TV last night.	She **is going to watch** TV tonight.
eat	Jennifer **eats** breakfast with her family every day.	She **ate** breakfast with her family today.	She **is going to eat** dinner with Keesha on Saturday.

For the simple past tense of most regular verbs, add *-ed* or *-d*.
  play → play**ed**
Irregular verbs have special forms:
  eat → **ate**

A Look at Jennifer's weekly planner in Vocabulary C. Imagine it is Wednesday afternoon at 12:00. Write sentences. Use the correct form of the verb.

1. Jennifer / dinner with her family / Monday
   <u>Jennifer ate dinner with her family on Monday.</u>

2. She / lunch / 12:00 / yesterday
   _____

3. Jennifer and Nathan / bus / every morning
   _____

4. Jennifer / soccer / Saturday
   _____

5. Jennifer and Keesha / relax / Saturday night
   _____

Adverbs of Frequency

always 100% of the time	usually	often	sometimes	hardly ever	never 0% of the time

B Rewrite the sentences. Add the correct adverbs from the reading on page 2.

1. Jennifer wakes up late.

   <u>Jennifer hardly ever wakes up late.</u>

2. Jennifer eats a healthy breakfast.

   _____

3. She has rice and fish.

   _____

4. Jennifer and Nathan are on time, but today they were late.

   _____

5. Jennifer loves her TV show and misses it.

   _____

ORGANIZATION

Chronological Order

Find each of the sequence words in the reading on page 2. Write the complete sentences.

1. First: _____

2. Then: _____

3. After that: _____

4. Finally: _____

Remember!

Chronological order tells about events in the order they happen. The reading on page 2 tells about Jennifer's day in time order. Times and days show chronological order. These sequence words also show time order: *before, first, after, next, then.*

   On Monday I woke up **at 7:00. First,** I ate breakfast **at 7:45. Then,** I went to school **at 8:30. After** school, I played soccer. **Next,** I ate dinner **at 6:45. Before** dinner, I watched TV.

WRITING STRATEGIES

Writing a Good Paragraph

Read the following paragraph. <u>Underline</u> the topic sentence. Circle the supporting sentences.

My Busy Day

I am very busy during the week. In the morning, I get ready for my busy day. First, I usually get up at 7:00. I take a quick shower and get dressed. Then, I eat breakfast with my family. Finally, at 8:00 I go to school. School is the most important part of my busy day. My sister and I go to the same school. In the morning, we have Spanish, math, and history. In the afternoon, we have English and science. My favorite subject is science. The fun part of my busy day is after school. My sister and I often play sports. At 5:00 in the evening we take a train home. Mom is there to help us make dinner. Then at 6:00, we do our homework. Dad usually comes home just before we go to bed. We usually go to bed early. We are tired after such a busy day.

WRITING CONVENTIONS

Punctuation

Add a comma or commas to each sentence.

1. This morning Jennifer got up early.

2. Then she ate breakfast with her family.

3. She had a piece of toast some fruit and a glass of milk.

4. At 8:00 A.M. she took the bus.

5. Right now it is 1:00 in the afternoon.

1. This morning, Jennifer got up early.

2.

Narrative Writing

Narration tells a story. It can describe a series of events or tell about one specific event. In narration paragraphs, the topic sentence introduces the story. The supporting sentences tell what happens in the story. The concluding sentence ends the story, summarizes the story, or tells why it is important. Journal entries and personal essays are examples of narrations.

 A Read. Read Caleb's journal entry.

My Busy Weekends

My weekends are usually really busy, but they are fun. Everyone in my family has different activities each weekend. We usually wake up early and eat breakfast at home. Sometimes we have a game or class in the afternoon. On Sunday, we always have a big dinner with my grandfather. Last Saturday was very busy. We went to my football game from 10:00 to 12:00. After the game, we ate lunch at our favorite restaurant. At 2:00, my brother and I went to our music lessons. I play the piano. My brother plays the violin. Then in the evening, we had a picnic in the park from 6:00 to 7:30. Next weekend is going to be very exciting. On Saturday, we are going to drive to Boston. We are going to go to a big party for my grandmother. She is going to be sixty years old. After the party, we are going to stay at my cousin's house. Next weekend is going to be busy, but it is going to be special.

Learn new words. Write them in your personal dictionary.

  B Write words and sentences. Complete the chart with Caleb's weekend activities. Use information from his journal entry. Then, complete the paragraph about Caleb.

Caleb's Weekend Activities

Usual Weekend Activities	Last Weekend's Activities	Next Weekend's Activities
1. *Caleb and his family usually wake up early and eat breakfast at home.*	**4.**	**8.**
2.	**5.**	**9.**
3.	**6.**	**10.**
	7.	

Caleb's weekends are usually really busy, but fun. Caleb and his family usually wake up early and eat breakfast at home. Sometimes they . . . .

STEP–BY–STEP WRITING

Purpose: Describe Daily Activities

WRITING PROMPT

Write a paragraph about your weekend activities. What do you usually do on the weekend? What did you do last weekend? What are you going to do next weekend?

✔ **Prompt Checklist**

❑ I read the prompt carefully.
❑ I understood what the prompt asks me to do.

STEP 1 Pre-write

Look at Caleb's three-column organizer. Think about the activities you are going to include in your narration. Copy the organizer or make one on a computer. Complete the organizer with information about your weekend activities.

Caleb's Three-Column Organizer

Usual Weekend Activities	Last Weekend's Activities	Next Weekend's Activities
Wake up early	Went to football game at 10 A.M.	Drive to Boston
Eat breakfast at home	Went out to lunch at favorite restaurant	Go to Grandma's party
Game or class	Went to music class at 2 P.M.	Stay at cousins' house
Dinner with grandfather	Ate picnic dinner in the park	

STEP 2 Organize

Look at Caleb's paragraph organizer. Copy the organizer or make one on a computer. Organize your topic, supporting and concluding sentences.

Caleb's Paragraph Organizer

Topic Sentence	My weekends are usually busy, but they are fun.
Supporting Sentence 1	Everyone in my family has different activities each weekend.
Supporting Sentence 2	Last Saturday was very busy.
Supporting Sentence 3	Next weekend is going to be very exciting.
Concluding Sentence	Next weekend is going to be busy, but it is going to be special.

STEP 3 Draft and Revise

A Practice. Look at Caleb's first draft. How can he improve it? Answer the questions.

My Busy Weekends

(1) Do you have busy weekends? (2) Everyone in my family has different activities each weekend. (3) We usually wake up early. (4) I often eat breakfast at home. (5) Sometimes we have a game or class in the afternoon. (6) On Sunday, we have a big dinner with my grandfather. (7) Last Saturday was very busy. (8) We went to my football game from 10:00 to 12:00. (9) At 2:00, my brother and I went to our music lessons. (10) After the game, we ate lunch at our favorite restaurant. (11) I play the piano. (12) My brother plays the violin. (13) Then in the evening, we had a picnic in the park from 6:00 to 7:30. (14) Next weekend is going to be very exciting. (15) On Saturday, we are going to drive to Boston. (16) We are going to go to a big birthday party for my grandmother. (17) She is going to be sixty years old. (18) We are going to stay at my cousins' house. (19) Are your weekends that busy?

1. Which would be a better topic sentence to introduce Caleb's narration?
   Ⓐ My weekends are usually really busy, but they are fun.
   B My name is Caleb Lehman.
   C Here is a description of my weekend.
   D People have relaxing weekends.

2. Which frequency adverb should Caleb add to sentence 6 to show that he has dinner with his grandfather every weekend?
   A sometimes
   B usually
   C often
   D always

3. What is a better order for sentences 8, 9, 10?
   A 9, 8, 10
   B 8, 10, 9
   C 10, 8, 9
   D 9, 10, 8

4. Which time order phrase could Caleb add to sentence 18 to show chronological order?
   A Before the party,
   B During the party,
   C At the party,
   D After the party,

B Draft. Write a first draft of your paragraph. Use your notes from Steps 1 and 2.

C Revise. Read your first draft. How can you improve it? Look at the revision checklist. Revise your writing.

✔ Revision Checklist

❑ I used chronological order and sequence words to show time order.
❑ My supporting sentences all relate to the topic sentence.
❑ My concluding sentence clearly ends my paragraph.

STEP 4 Edit

A **Practice. Look at the sentences. Choose the best substitute for the <u>underlined</u> words. If the sentence is correct, choose "Make no change."**

1. I <u>came</u> up at 7:00 this morning.
   A get
   Ⓑ got
   C wake
   D Make no change.

2. We <u>take</u> a trip to Florida last year.
   A took
   B taking
   C takes
   D Make no change.

3. My friends <u>come</u> to my house every day.
   A coming
   B comes
   C came
   D Make no change.

4. <u>Diego and Miles is</u> going to come to my party.
   A Diego and Miles are
   B Diego and Miles is not
   C They is
   D Make no change.

5. I play soccer <u>at</u> Mondays.
   A for
   B on
   C to
   D Make no change.

6. She eats lunch <u>at</u> 12:00 to 1:00.
   A in
   B from
   C on
   D Make no change.

B **Edit. Reread your draft from Step 3. Look at the editing checklist. Edit your writing.**

C **Peer Edit. Exchange drafts with a partner. Tell your partner what you like about the draft. Look at the editing checklist. Tell your partner how to improve the draft.**

STEP 5 Publish

Write your paragraph in your best handwriting or use a computer. Look at Caleb's paragraph on page 11 for ideas. Present your narrative paragraph to the class.

✔ Editing Checklist

my		
me	partner	
☐	☐	used sequence words, time phrases, and frequency adverbs correctly
☐	☐	used simple verb tense correctly
☐	☐	used correct spelling, punctuation, and capitalization

TECHNOLOGY

Researching Online Daily Planners

 Go to an Internet search engine. Do a keyword search for "free daily planner." Click (SEARCH). How many free daily planners are available online? Click on a hyperlink for a daily planner Web site. Evaluate three different daily planners. What do you like about each planner? What don't you like about each planner? Make lists. Cite your sources. Write down the Web page title, the Web site title, the publication date, the access date, and the URL for each Web site.

Unit 2

Describe a Friend

UNIT OBJECTIVES

Writing
descriptive writing

Organization
main idea and supporting details

Writing Strategies
signal and connecting words

Writing Conventions
compound sentences

Vocabulary
predicate adjectives
synonyms and antonyms

Grammar
be going to vs. *will*

Technology
researching people online

Descriptive Paragraphs

A Discuss. Do these words describe appearance or personality? Write the words in the correct column.

thin	pretty	kind	relaxed	silly
strong	funny	quiet	helpful	straight-haired
~~serious~~	shy	tall	~~average build~~	handsome

Appearance	Personality
average build	serious

 B Read. Read Jennifer's description of her friend, Keesha.

My Friend, Keesha

Keesha is one of my good friends. I met her on the first day of school last year. It was my first day in a new school and a new town. I was nervously trying to open my locker. Then, Keesha came over and showed me how to open the lock. After that, she was my hero. We became friends that day.

Keesha has a great personality and is very pretty too. She is sixteen years old. She is five feet, two inches tall. Her face is long and thin. Her eyes are dark brown, and her hair is curly and black. She smiles a lot. Keesha also stays in shape. She is not heavy or thin. She has an average build. She plays soccer and dances. She doesn't like to dress up. She usually wears jeans and T-shirts. Keesha has a wonderful personality. She is funny, but she is also very sensitive. She can make me smile even when I'm having a bad day. She always cheers me up. She is an amazing person.

Keesha plans to be a teacher in the future. She loves science, so she is going to be a science teacher. I think that she will be an excellent teacher. I know this because she often helps me with my homework. I think her students will learn a lot from her. She is going to go to college in California after high school. I will miss her very much. Keesha is a good person and a great friend.

 C Write captions. Write a sentence for each picture on page 15. Use sentences from the reading.

1. <u>Keesha is one of my good friends.</u>

2. _____

3. _____

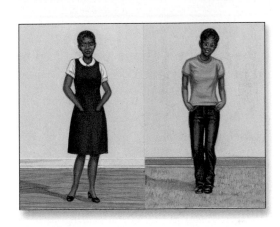

4. _____

5. _____

6. _____

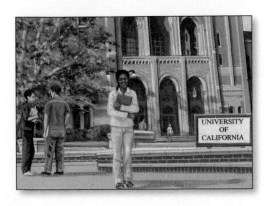

7. _____

8. _____

A Find each word in the reading on page 14. Look at the words around it to guess the meaning. Compare your answers with a partner.

Nouns	Verbs	Adverbs	Adjectives	Expressions
college	meet	nervously	dark	cheer up
future	show		heavy	dress up
personality	smile		sensitive	in shape

Learn new words. Write them in your personal dictionary.

B Complete the sentences about Keesha and her family. The adjective placement is different in each sentence.

1. Keesha has black, wavy hair.
   Her <u>hair is black and wavy.</u>_____ .

2. Keesha's brothers have brown eyes.
   Their _____ .

3. Keesha and her mother have dark hair.
   Their _____ .

4. Her father's smile is nice.
   He _____ .

5. Keesha's personality is great.
   She _____ .

Remember!
Adjectives describe or give information about nouns. **Predicate adjectives** follow **linking verbs** like *is*. Predicate adjectives are used differently than adjectives placed before the noun.

Keesha **has** a → Keesha's face **is** *long, thin* face.   *long* and *thin*.

C Find the words from the box in the reading on page 14. Complete the chart with the synonyms and antonyms. Then, write complete sentences.

average	dark	heavy	~~amazing~~
sensitive	future	wavy	in shape
~~good~~	wonderful		

Remember!
Synonyms are words that have a similar meaning. **Antonyms** are words that have the opposite meaning. Good writers use many different words to make their writing interesting.

synonyms   very big = huge
antonyms   tall ≠ short

Synonyms		Antonyms	
very interesting	1. ___amazing___	bad	6. ___good___
normal	2. _____	careless	7. _____
great	3. _____	past	8. _____
overweight	4. _____	light-colored	9. _____
physically fit	5. _____	straight	10. _____

A The sentences below are not true. Write true sentences about Keesha. Use information from the reading on page 14.

Simple Future Tense with *be going to*	
Affirmative	**Negative**
Keesha **is going to be** a teacher.	She **is not going to live** in New York.
We **are going to go** to different colleges.	I **am not going to go** to college in California.

Simple Future Tense with *will*	
Affirmative	**Negative**
Keesha **will be** an excellent teacher.	She **will not be** a bad teacher.
Her students **will learn** a lot from her.	I **will not forget** Keesha.

Use *be going to* to express a definite plan. Use *will* to express a promise. Use both *be going to* or *will* to express a prediction.

Contractions
will not = won't

1. Keesha is going to be an English teacher.
   <u>Keesha is not going to be an English teacher. She is going to be a science teacher.</u>

2. Keesha will be a bad teacher.
   _____

3. Keesha's students are going to learn very little from her.
   _____

4. Keesha is going to go to college in New York.
   _____

5. Jennifer will miss Keesha a little.
   _____

B Write sentences in the future tense using *going to* or *will*.

1. My friend Braeden / be / a doctor (definite plan)
   <u>My friend Braeden is going to be a doctor.</u>

2. He / be / a great doctor (prediction)
   _____

3. He / go / to Columbia University / next year (definite plan)
   _____

4. I / call / him every week (promise)
   _____

5. He / be / busy (prediction)
   _____

ORGANIZATION

Main Idea and Supporting Details

Reread paragraph 2 on page 14. Complete the chart with three minor supporting sentences for each main supporting sentence.

Topic Sentence	Keesha has a great personality and is very pretty, too.
Main Supporting Sentences	**Minor Supporting Sentences**
She is sixteen years old.	1. She is five feet, two inches tall. 2. _____ 3. _____
Keesha also stays in shape.	4. _____ 5. _____ 6. _____
Keesha has a wonderful personality.	7. _____ 8. _____ 9. _____
Concluding Sentence	She is an amazing person.

WRITING STRATEGIES

Signal and Connecting Words

Change each sentence. Use the signal or connecting word in parentheses to make compound sentences.

Remember!

Use signal words to add information. Use connecting words to connect ideas or sentences. Use a comma after most signal and connecting words.

signal words	*after that, finally, as well, too, then, also*
connecting words	*and, but, or, so, because*

1. (and) It was my first day in a new school. It was my first day in a new town.

2. (then) I was nervously trying to open my locker. Keesha came over.

3. (or) She isn't heavy. She isn't thin.

4. (but) She is funny. She is also very sensitive.

5. (so) She loves science. She is going to be a science teacher.

6. (because) I know this. She often helps me with my homework.

1. It was my first day in a new school and in a new town.

WRITING CONVENTIONS

Compound Sentences

Add punctuation to these sentences.

1. Jennifer and her brother take the bus to school

2. Keesha makes me smile and cheers me up

3. Her eyes are dark brown and her hair is wavy and black

4. She is a good person and has a great personality

5. She came over helped me study and was amazing

6. He loves soccer so he is going to be a P.E. teacher

Remember!

Compound subjects are two or more subjects in a sentence. Compound verbs are two or more verbs in a sentence. Use commas if there are more than two subjects or verbs. Compound sentences are two or more complete sentences combined with a connecting word. Use a comma before the connecting word.

compound subject	**Jennifer** and **Keesha** are friends.
compound verb	Keesha **plays soccer, dances,** and **smiles** a lot.
compound sentence	She loves science, **so she is going to be a science teacher.**

Descriptive Writing

> **Descriptive writing** gives details and information about a topic. A **biographical description** can describe how a person looks, acts, what they like, and what they mean to the writer. Biographies and stories often use descriptive writing.

 A **Read.** Read Lisha's biographical description of her friend, Carlos.

Learn new words. Write them in your personal dictionary.

My Friend, Carlos

Carlos Herrera is a friend from school, and he is also my best friend. He is sixteen years old. He is going to be seventeen next month. Carlos is very handsome. He is five feet, six inches tall. His eyes are brown, and his face is round. His hair is brown and curly. He wears glasses and jeans every day. Carlos has a wonderful personality. He is a serious person, but he also likes to have fun. He is very smart, too. He is a good student, and he gets good grades. He is patient and kind. Carlos has many hobbies. He likes to draw and play the guitar. His favorite activity is skateboarding. He and his friends skateboard every day after school. He even skates in competitions. He has won many first place prizes. All of these things make Carlos a very interesting person.

Carlos talks a lot about the future. He is going to graduate from high school this year. He plans to work while he goes to college. He says that working will help him pay for college. He thinks he will study architecture, but he does not know for sure. I know that he will be successful because he studies and works hard. He will have a lot fun in the future, too.

B **Write Paragraphs.** Look at the pictures on page 21. Write the correct paragraph from Lisha's biography under each picture.

Descriptive Paragraphs

_____

_____

_____

_____

_____

_____

_____

_____

_____

STEP-BY-STEP WRITING

Purpose: Describe a Friend

WRITING PROMPT

Think of one of your good friends. What does the person look like? What does the person like to do? What do you think he or she will do in the future? Write one paragraph describing your friend's appearance, personality, and hobbies. Write another paragraph describing your friend's future plans and your predictions for his or her future.

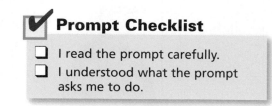 **Prompt Checklist**

❏ I read the prompt carefully.
❏ I understood what the prompt asks me to do.

STEP 1 Pre-write

Look at Lisha's word web. Think about the information you need for your description. Draw the web or make one on a computer. Complete it with information for your paragraphs.

Lisha's Word Web

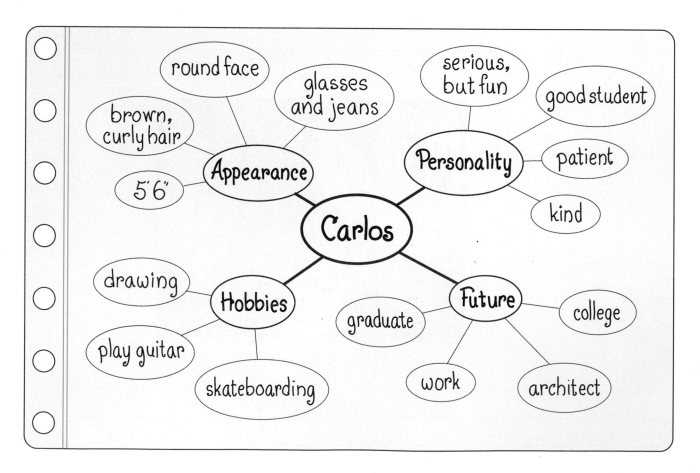

STEP 2 Organize

Look at Lisha's Main Idea and Details organizer. Complete the organizer below with ideas for your biography.

Lisha's Main Idea and Details Organizer	
Main Idea	**Details**
Carlos is very handsome.	• He is 5 feet, 6 inches tall. • His eyes are brown, and his face is round. • His hair is brown and curly. • He wears glasses and jeans every day.
Carlos has a wonderful personality.	• He is serious, but fun. • He is a good student. • He is patient and kind.
Carlos has many hobbies.	• He likes to draw and play the guitar. • His favorite activity is skateboarding.
Carlos talks a lot about the future.	• He is going to graduate this year. • He is going to work and go to college. • He will study architecture.

Main Idea and Details organizer	
Main Ideas	**Details**
	• • •
	• • •
	• • •
	• • •

DO NOT WRITE IN THIS BOOK

STEP 3 Draft and Revise

A **Practice. Look at Lisha's first draft. How can she improve it? Answer the questions on page 25.**

LISHA'S FIRST DRAFT

My Friend, Carlos

(1) Carlos Herrera is a friend from school. (2) He is also my best friend. (3) He is sixteen years old. (4) He is going to be seventeen next month. (5) He is 5 feet, 6 inches tall. (6) His eyes are brown and his face is round. (7) His hair is brown and curly. (8) He wears glasses and jeans every day. (9) Carlos has a wonderful personality. (10) He is a serious person but he also likes to have fun. (11) He is very smart, too. (12) He is a good student, and he gets good grades. (13) He is patient and kind. (14) Carlos has many hobbies. (15) His favorite activity is skateboarding. (16) He and his friends skateboard every day after school. (17) He even skates in competitions. (18) He has won many first place prizes.

(19) Carlos talks a lot about the future. (20) He is going to graduate from high school this year. (21) He plans to work while he goes to college. (22) He says that working will help him pay for college. (23) He thinks he will study architecture but he does not know for sure. (24) I know that he will be successful, because he studies and works hard. (25) He will have a lot fun in the future, too.

1. How can Lisha best rewrite sentences 1 and 2 of paragraph 1 with a connecting word?

   A Carlos Herrera is a friend from school, he is also my best friend.

   B Carlos Herrera is a friend from school, so he is also my best friend.

   Ⓒ Carlos Herrera is a friend from school, and he is also my best friend.

   D Carlos Herrera is a friend from school, then he is also my best friend.

2. Where should Lisha put a comma in sentence 10?

   A He is a serious person but he also, likes to have fun.

   B He is a serious person but, he also likes to have fun.

   C He is a serious person, but he also likes to have fun.

   D He is a serious person but he, also likes to have fun.

3. Which is the best concluding sentence for paragraph 1?

   A Carlos does not like to dress up.

   B All of these qualities make Carlos a very interesting person.

   C I am learning to skateboard, too.

   D Don't you agree that Carlos is handsome?

4. Which supporting detail can Lisha add after sentence 14 in paragraph 1?

   A He likes to draw and play the guitar.

   B He wears glasses.

   C He teaches his little brother how to skateboard.

   D He is going to get a good job someday.

5. Which is the best topic sentence for paragraph 2?

   A Carlos is very handsome.

   B Carlos talks a lot about the future.

   C Carlos has a wonderful personality.

   D Carlos is a great person.

6. How can Lisha correctly punctuate sentence 23?

   A He thinks he will study architecture, but he does not know for sure.

   B He thinks he will study architecture but he does not know for sure!

   C He thinks he will study architecture but he does not know for sure?

   D He thinks, he will study architecture but, he does not know for sure.

B **Draft. Write a first draft for your description. Use your notes from Steps 1 and 2.**

C **Revise. Read your first draft. How can you improve it? Look at the revision checklist. Revise your writing.**

✔ **Revision Checklist**

❑ I used strong descriptive adjectives to describe my friend.

❑ I used signal and connecting words for clear compound sentences.

❑ I included topic, supporting, and concluding sentences in each paragraph.

STEP 4 Edit

A Practice. Look at the sentences. Choose the best word or phrase to complete each sentence.

1. Ashley _____ a trip last month.
   A take
   B takes
   Ⓒ took
   D is taking

2. We _____ baseball every day.
   A play
   B plays
   C playing
   D players

3. They _____ watch a movie tomorrow night.
   A is going to
   B are going to
   C is watching
   D watched

4. She _____ eats dinner with her family.
   A is
   B are
   C usually
   D will

5. I think Davis and Anita _____ enjoy college next year.
   A is going to
   B will
   C are
   D should

6. My friends and I are going to go shopping _____ are going to have fun.
   A , and we
   B . My friends and I
   C , my friends and I
   D . And we

B Edit. Reread your draft from Step 3. Look at the editing checklist. Edit your writing.

C Peer Edit. Exchange drafts with a partner. Tell your partner what you like about the draft. Look at the editing checklist. Tell your partner how to improve the draft.

STEP 5 Publish

Write your paragraphs in your best handwriting or use a computer. Look at Lisha's paragraphs on page 20 for ideas. Present your paragraphs to the class.

✔ Editing Checklist

me	my partner	
❏	❏	used different and interesting adjectives correctly to describe my friend
❏	❏	used future with *be going to* and *will* correctly
❏	❏	used signal and connecting words correctly
❏	❏	used correct punctuation for compound sentences
❏	❏	used correct spelling and capitalization

TECHNOLOGY

Researching People Online

Think of a famous person you admire. Go to an online search engine. Do a keyword search for "biography of (the person's name)." Use quotes around the whole phrase. Use the research information to write a paragraph about the person. Describe the person's looks, personality, and hobbies (if listed). Cite your sources. Share your research with the class.

GROUP WRITING

WRITING PROMPT

Work in a group to write about one of these topics. Follow the steps below.

1. Choose your topic.
2. Read the person's information.
3. Write a first draft.
4. Revise and edit the draft with your group.
5. Present your group's paragraph to the class.

Topic 1

Sandy is on vacation this week and she's having fun. Today is Wednesday. Write a narrative paragraph. What did Sandy do on Monday and Tuesday? What is she doing today? What is she going to do on Thursday and Friday?

Sandy's Vacation Week Planner

Time	Monday	Tuesday	Wednesday	Thursday	Friday
8:00 A.M.	Eat breakfast in the hotel		Eat breakfast in the hotel		Go to the train station
10:00 A.M.	Go to the beach	Eat breakfast in a restaurant	Rest by the pool	Eat breakfast in a restaurant	Take train to the airport
12:00 P.M.	Eat a picnic lunch on the beach	Go shopping	Go to a museum	Go to a show	Fly home
2:00 P.M.		Rest in the hotel	Eat a late lunch at a restaurant	Relax by the pool	

Topic 2

Write a biographical paragraph about Jason Fields. Use information from his student ID and his yearbook page. Write about his appearance, personality, and future plans.

HENRY PUBLIC SCHOOL
STUDENT IDENTIFICATION
NAME: Jason Fields
Age: 15 years old

Jason Fields

Signature

JASON FIELDS
Awards: Best Personality,
Most Valuable Player in Football,
Funniest Kid in Class
Hobbies: football, reading, and playing guitar
Future Goals: go to college; be a coach
play football in college; be a coach

TIMED WRITING

Choose one writing task. Complete the task in 45 minutes.

WRITING PROMPT 1

Describe an important event in your week. Write a narrative paragraph about an important event that occurred or will occur this week. Write about a sporting event, a party, or a holiday. Tell about the event, what you did, and what you will do next time. Write three or more sentences about each topic.

Test Tip

Prewrite! After you read the prompt, write down all the ideas you have for the passage. Next, use a graphic organizer (web, outline, etc.) to organize your ideas. Then, you will be ready to write.

WRITING PROMPT 2

Write a biography about a person in your family. Tell about their appearance, their personality, their future plans, and why they are important to you. Write three or more sentences about each topic.

SELF–CHECK

Think about your writing skills. Check (✔) the answers that are true.

1. I understand . . .
   - ❏ daily activity phrases.
   - ❏ times and days.
   - ❏ appearance and personality adjectives.

2. I can correctly use . . .
   - ❏ synonyms and antonyms.
   - ❏ predicate adjectives.
   - ❏ appearance and personality adjectives.

3. I can correctly use . . .
   - ❏ future tense with *going to.*
   - ❏ connecting words.
   - ❏ sequence words.
   - ❏ future tense with *will.*
   - ❏ simple past and present tenses.
   - ❏ frequency adverbs.

4. I remember that a good paragraph . . .
   - ❏ is indented.
   - ❏ has a topic sentence.
   - ❏ has major and minor supporting sentences.
   - ❏ has a concluding sentence.

5. I can correctly . . .
   - ❏ use signal and connecting words.
   - ❏ punctuate sentences and paragraphs.
   - ❏ write compound sentences.

6. I can organize my writing by . . .
   - ❏ time.
   - ❏ main idea and supporting details.

7. I can write to . . .
   - ❏ narrate.
   - ❏ describe.

Unit 3

Write a Friendly Message

UNIT OBJECTIVES

Writing
writing a friendly letter or e-mail

Organization
spatial order

Writing Strategies
spatial description

Writing Conventions
greetings and closings

Vocabulary
sensory adjectives
letter-writing expressions
weather

Grammar
present vs. past continuous tense
there was/were
quantity adjectives

Technology
finding e-mail pen pals

A **Discuss. Close your eyes and think about what you did yesterday. Answer the questions. Then, describe the scene to your partner. Use sensory details.**

1. Where were you? _____

2. What did you see there? _____

3. What did you smell there? _____

4. What did you hear there? _____

5. What did you feel there? _____

B **Read. Read Jennifer's letter.**

October 11, 2008

Dear Mei,

How are you? I am thinking of you today. I feel homesick. I often think of you and all of my friends in China. I miss everyone. I am sitting at my desk and looking out the window. It is raining here in New York. Outside, there are many people on the sidewalk. All of them are wearing coats and carrying umbrellas. Everyone is hurrying because it's such a rainy day. I am very happy to be dry now. I was not feeling happy earlier. I had some bad luck this afternoon.

After school, my friend Keesha and I were walking to a restaurant. We wanted a snack. A lot of buses and cars were driving up and down the street. One of the cars went through a puddle of water and splashed me. I was upset and cold. We ran to the restaurant. Inside the restaurant, it was loud, but warm. I felt a little better. Keesha and I sat down. Keesha looked into her backpack and took out her gym towel. She gave it to me. That was really nice of her! The towel was scratchy on my face. It smelled clean and fresh. I was happy to be dry. Keesha and I looked around the restaurant. There was a family by the window. There were many men and women at the counter. There were a few desserts on the counter. There was some apple pie, too. Keesha and I ate a piece of pie. The apples were sweet, and the crust was salty. It was great! I was finally all warm and dry. In the end, Keesha and I laughed about when the car splashed me. I love being with Keesha. She is a really great friend.

I hope you are well. Are you learning English? Can you read my letter? I hope you are not having difficulty in school. Did you like my story? Please write soon. My parents send their best to your parents.

Your friend,
Jennifer

 C **Write captions. Write a sentence for each picture on page 31. Use sentences from the reading.**

1. <u>I am sitting in my bedroom</u>
   <u>and looking out the window.</u>

2. _____

3. _____

4. _____

5. _____

6. _____

7. _____

8. _____

9. _____

10. _____

11. _____

VOCABULARY

A Find each word in the reading on page 30. Look at the words around it to guess the meaning. Compare your answers with a partner.

Nouns	Adjectives		Expressions
coat	clean	scratchy	I hope you are well.
towel	dry	warm	In the end,
sidewalk	fresh	homesick	send (someone) their best
umbrella	rainy	upset	Your friend,
Verbs	salty	well	
rain			
splash			

Learn new words. Write them in your personal dictionary.

B What do these sensory adjectives describe in the reading on page 30? Write the words in the correct columns.

~~warm~~	cold	dry	scratchy	sweet	clean
little	salty	fresh	loud	rainy	

Remember!
You can use sensory adjectives to add details. Sensory adjectives describe how something looks, feels, tastes, or smells.

How does it . . .

look? 👁	sound? 👂	feel? ✋	taste? 👄	smell? 👃
		warm		

C Complete the sentences about Jennifer's day. Use the correct form of the words in the box.

sidewalk	upset	~~rain~~	coat	splash	umbrella

(1) It _____rained_____ all day in New York. (2) Everyone wore _____.

(3) Everyone carried _____. (4) Jennifer and Keesha walked on the _____

to go to a restaurant. (5) A car drove through a puddle and _____ Jennifer.

(6) Jennifer felt _____.

Continuous Tenses	
Present Continuous Tense	**Past Continuous Tense**
I **am thinking** of you today. Everyone **is hurrying** to get to a dry place.	Keesha and I **were walking** to a restaurant. Buses and cars **were driving** up and down the street.
I hope you **are not having** difficulty in school.	I **was not feeling** happy earlier.

Use the **present continuous** to describe an event that is happening in the present. Use the **past continuous** to describe an event that started, continued for a while, and ended in the past.

Contractions

aren't = are not

wasn't = was not

A What was everyone doing yesterday? Change the sentences to the past continuous tense.

1. It is raining.
   It was raining.

2. Jennifer and Keesha are walking to the restaurant.

   _____

3. Cars are driving up and down the street.

   _____

4. Jennifer is standing by the road.

   _____

5. Jennifer and Keesha are laughing.

   _____

6. Jennifer is writing Mei a letter.

   _____

Statements with *There was / There were*		
	Affirmative	**Negative**
Singular	**There was** some apple pie.	**There was not any** apple pie.
Plural	**There were** men and women at the counter.	**There were not any** men and women at the counter.

B Complete the sentences below by writing *There was* or *There were*.

1. _____ cars and buses driving up and down the street.

2. _____ many people on the sidewalk.

3. _____ a few desserts on the counter.

4. _____ warm apple pie for Jennifer and Keesha.

5. _____ not any ice cream.

Contractions

wasn't = was not

weren't = were not

Quantity adjectives tell how much of something there is.

<—all of ———many / a lot ———some ——a few —a little——one of ———no / not any—>

C Find each quantity adjective in the reading on page 30. Write the complete sentences. Then, rewrite each sentence, replacing the quantity adjective. Notice how the meaning changes.

a lot	many	all of	a little	one of	a few

1. Outside, there are many people on the sidewalk.
   Outside, there are a few people on the sidewalk.

2. _____

3. _____

4. _____

5. _____

6. _____

WRITING STRATEGIES

Spatial Description

Complete the sentences from the reading with the correct preposition. Use each word only once.

to	inside	by
through	around	up

Remember!
Spatial descriptions often use prepositions or prepositional phrases. They tell where something is located or where an action takes place.
I'm sitting **at** my desk and looking **out** my window.

1. Keesha and I were walking _____ to _____ a restaurant.

2. A lot of buses and cars were driving _____ and down the street.

3. One of the cars went _____ a puddle of water and splashed me.

4. _____ the restaurant, it was loud, but warm.

5. Keesha and I looked _____ the restaurant.

6. There was a family _____ the window.

34 Step–by–Step Writing Book 2

WRITING CONVENTIONS

Greetings and Closings

Correct the following greetings and closings.
Write two more greetings and closings on the lines.

1. Dear, Felipe _____

2. Hello Jennifer _____

3. To my friend Ann Marie _____

4. From James, _____

5. Yours Lisa _____

6. All the best Jason, _____

7. _____

8. _____

Remember!
Friendly letters use informal language.
Greetings and closings are informal
and familiar. Both greetings and
closings are followed by commas. In a
greeting, the comma comes after the
addressee's name. In a closing, the
comma comes before the sender's
name. All words in greetings and
closings are capitalized.
For example:
Dear Sarah, / Hello Sarah, / Fondly,
Jesse / Your Friend, Jesse

ORGANIZATION

Spatial Order

Number the sentences in spatial order. Then, write
the sentences in the correct order.

Remember!
You can use spatial order to describe
a place. Spatial order gives information
by location or the way the writer sees
places. In the reading on page 30,
Jennifer describes the restaurant the
way she is seeing it.

Group 1

_____ A lot of buses and cars were driving up and down the street.

_____ We ran to the restaurant.

_1_ After school, my friend Keesha and I were walking to a restaurant.

_____ Keesha and I sat down.

_____ Inside the restaurant, it was loud, but warm.

_____ One of the cars went through a puddle of water and splashed me.

Group 2

_____ There were a few desserts on the counter.

_____ There was a family by the window.

_____ There were many men and women at the counter.

_____ There was some apple pie, too.

_____ Keesha and I looked around the restaurant.

Writing a Friendly Letter or E-mail

In a friendly letter or e-mail, the author writes an informal message to a friend or family member. The heading gives the date of the letter. The greeting says hello to the receiver. The body often tells about the author and recent activities or events. The author may also ask the receiver questions to end the letter. The closing says "goodbye" before the signature.

 A Read. Read Antonio's e-mail to a friend.

Learn new words. Write them in your personal dictionary.

From: Antonio Rojas (arojas@h-net.com)   **Sent:** June 12, 2008
To: Eduardo Cardenas (ecardenas@t-com.net)
Subject: Hi there!

Hi Eduardo,

    How are you? I am fine. It is Saturday afternoon and I am sitting in an Internet café. It is a hot summer day in New Orleans. I am sitting at a small round table near the door of the café. I am eating ice cream and thinking of you.

    I had a very interesting morning. I went to the park. It was a really hot day. There were many people at the park. A few people were walking their dogs. Some children were playing and running around. There was a dry fountain in the middle of the park. It doesn't work and it is usually dry. The fountain looked shady and cool. I sat down in the middle of the fountain. I wanted to relax. Suddenly, the fountain turned on. Water was everywhere! I was surprised and happy. I was wet, but I was cool. My friends came over to the fountain, too. They were helping me out of the fountain, but soon they were wet, too. Finally we were all playing in the fountain! We laughed and splashed each other. It was fun.

    I have good friends here, but I miss you and my friends in Puebla. I hope you are well and happy. When will you come to New Orleans for a visit? I want you to meet my friend, Maria. Roberto sends his best. Please write soon. Write to me in English!

Your friend,
Antonio

 B Write a Letter. Rewrite Antonio's e-mail to Eduardo as a friendly letter. Use the format on page 37.

A Letter to Eduardo

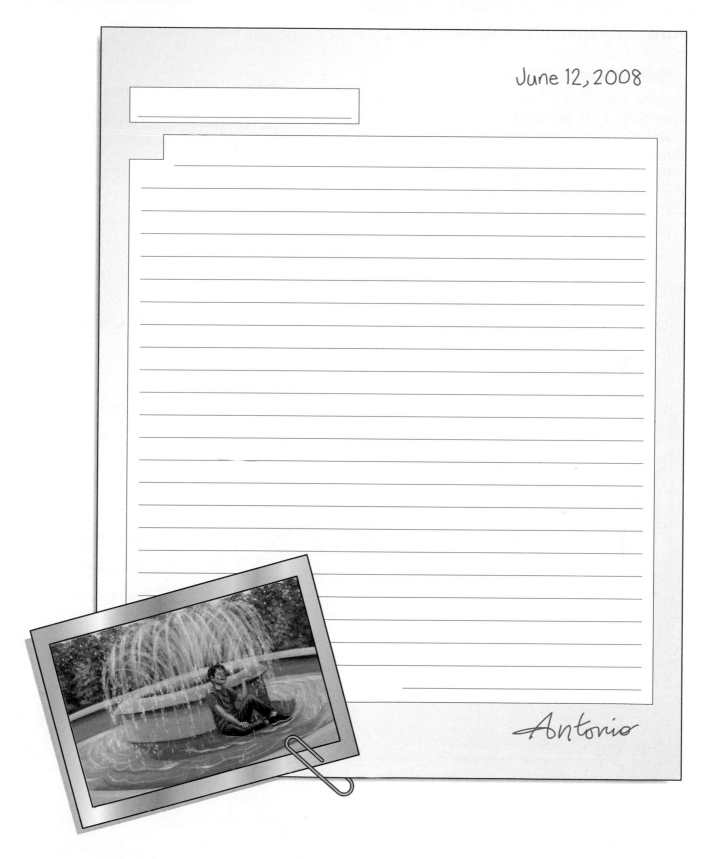

June 12, 2008

Antonio

STEP–BY–STEP WRITING

Purpose: Write a Friendly Message

WRITING PROMPT

Write a letter or e-mail to a friend or family member. First, tell the person how you are, where you are, and what you are doing. Then, tell a story about an important or funny event that happened recently. Use spatial description and sensory adjectives to describe the events. Finally, ask questions or make requests to the person to close the letter.

✔ **Prompt Checklist**

❑ I read the prompt carefully.
❑ I understood what the prompt asks me to do.

STEP 1 Pre-write

Look at Antonio's cluster map. Copy the cluster map or make one on a computer. Complete the cluster map with information for your friendly letter.

Antonio's Cluster Map

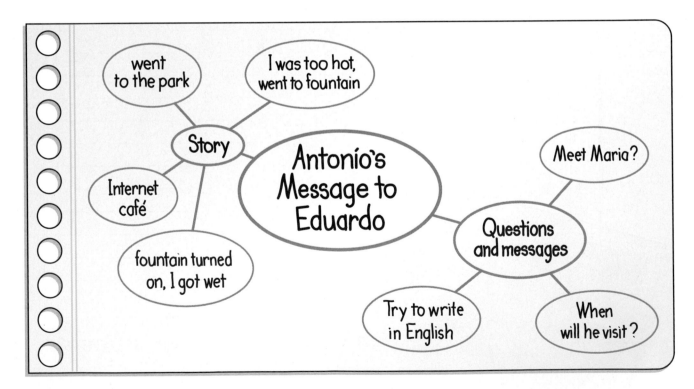

STEP 2 Organize

Look at Antonio's message outline. Organize your ideas. Complete the outline below with notes for your message.

Antonio's Message Outline

Greeting	Dear Eduardo,
Body	**Me:** I'm fine. I'm at a table in an Internet café, eating ice cream . . .
	Story: This morning I went to the park . . .
	Questions: When will he come visit? Will he write in English?
Closing	Your friend

Message Outline

Greeting	
Body	Me:
	Story:
	Questions:
Closing	

STEP 3 Draft and Revise

A Practice. Look at Antonio's first draft of the body of his message. How can he improve it? Answer the questions.

ANTONIO'S FIRST DRAFT

From: Antonio Rojas (arojas@h-net.com)   **Sent:** June 12, 2008

To: Eduardo Cardenas (ecardenas@t-com.net)

Subject: Hi there!

(1) Hi Eduardo,

(2) I am fine. (3) It is Saturday afternoon and I am sitting in an Internet café. (4) It is a hot summer day in New Orleans. (5) I am sitting at a small round table. (6) I am eating ice cream and thinking of you.

(7) I had a very interesting morning. (8) I went to the park. (9) It was a really hot day. (10) There were many people at the park. (11) People were walking their dogs. (12) Some children were playing and running around. (13) There was a dry fountain in the middle of the park. (14) It doesn't work and it is usually dry. (15) The fountain looked nice. (16) I sat down in the middle of the fountain. (17) I wanted to relax. (18) Suddenly, the fountain turned on. (19) Water was everywhere! (20) I was surprised and happy. (21) I was wet, but I was cool. (22) My friends came over to the fountain, too. (23) They were helping me out of the fountain, but soon they were wet, too. (24) Finally, we were all playing in the fountain! (25) We laughed and splashed each other. (26) It was fun.

(27) I have good friends here, but I miss you and my friends in Puebla. (28) I hope you are well and happy. (29) I want you to meet my friend, Maria. (30) Roberto sends his best. (31) Please write soon. (32) Write to me in English!

1. What letter convention did Antonio forget?

   A the date
   B the greeting
   C the body
   D the closing

2. What letter expression can Antonio write before sentence 2 to begin the message?

   A How are you?
   B Roberto says to tell you "Hello."
   C Your friend,
   D Please write soon.

3. What spatial phrase can Antonio add to sentence 5 to help the receiver see the scene?

   A on the counter of the café
   B in the sidewalk
   C to the park
   D near the door of the café

4. What quantity adjective can Antonio add to sentence 11 to make it more accurate?

   A all of the
   B one of the
   C a few
   D none of the

5. How can Antonio BEST replace "nice" in sentence 15 with stronger sensory adjectives?

   A good and clean
   B dirty and crowded
   C shady and cool
   D hot and uncomfortable

6. What's the BEST question Antonio could ask before sentence 29?

   A When will you come to New Orleans for a visit?
   B Did you like my story?
   C How is your family?
   D I can't wait to meet your friend.

B **Draft. Write a first draft of your friendly letter or e-mail. Use your notes from Steps 1 and 2.**

C **Revise. Read your first draft. How can you improve it? Look at the revision checklist. Revise your writing.**

✔ Revision Checklist

- ❏ I described my feelings, location, and activity.
- ❏ I told a story.
- ❏ I used spatial description and sensory adjectives to describe the events.
- ❏ I asked questions or made requests to the receiver.

STEP 4 Edit

A Practice. Look at the sentences. Choose the best substitute for the underlined words. If the sentence is correct, choose "Make no change."

1. I did my homework <u>inside</u> my desk.

   A by
   B at *(circled)*
   C to
   D Make no change.

2. My sister reads <u>in</u> her room.

   A on
   B at
   C to
   D Make no change.

3. It <u>snowed</u> outside right now!

   A are snowing
   B is snowing
   C was snowing
   D Make no change.

4. There <u>was</u> many dogs in the park.

   A wasn't
   B were
   C is
   D Make no change.

5. Yesterday, we <u>were wait</u> all day for her call.

   A are wait
   B are waiting
   C were waiting
   D Make no change.

6. There are <u>a few</u> people in the world.

   A some
   B not many
   C many
   D no

B Edit. Reread your draft from Step 3. Look at the editing checklist. Edit your writing.

C Peer edit. Exchange drafts with a partner. Tell your partner what you like about the draft. Look at the editing checklist. Tell your partner how to improve the draft.

STEP 5 Publish

Write your friendly letter or e-mail in your best handwriting or use a computer. Look at Antonio's e-mail and letter on pages 36 and 37 for ideas. Present your friendly letter or e-mail to the class.

✔ Editing Checklist

me	my partner	
❑	❑	used spatial words and sensory and quantity adjectives correctly
❑	❑	used the present and past continuous correctly
❑	❑	used *there was/there were* correctly
❑	❑	used correct spelling, punctuation, and capitalization

TECHNOLOGY

Finding E-mail Pen Pals

You can make friends around the world. Do a keyword search for "free e-mail pen pals." Click on a hyperlink. (Do not click on advertisements.) Have your parents or a teacher check the e-mail pen pal site to make sure it is safe. Then, follow the site directions to sign up for an e-mail pen pal. Never give your address, phone number, or other personal information to an e-mail pen pal.

Unit 4

Explain Directions

UNIT OBJECTIVES

Writing
technical writing

Organization
sequential order

Writing Strategies
pronoun reference

Writing Conventions
homonyms

Vocabulary
nouns for places
direction verbs and
phrases

Grammar
imperative sentences
modals: *can, should, must*

Technology
using map Web sites

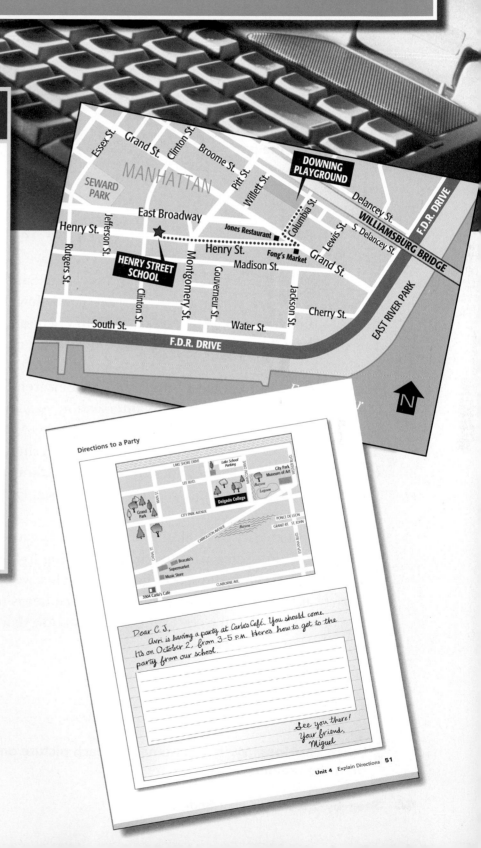

Directions to a Party

Dear C. J.,
    Avri is having a party at Carla's Café. You should come.
It's on October 2, from 3–5 P.M. Here's how to get to the
party from our school.

See you there!
Your friend,
Miguel

A **Discuss.** What are five interesting places near your school? Make a list. Compare your list with a partner.

1. _____

2. _____

3. _____

4. _____

5. _____

B **Read.** Read the party invitation.

August 26, 2008

Hello Everybody,

It is Nathan's birthday and we are going to have a party for him. Come to the Downing Playground for a soccer party on Saturday, September 22. The party is going to be from 12 P.M. to 4 P.M. Follow the directions below to get to the park. You can come from Henry School to the park on foot. You can come from your house if you know the location of our school.

First, from the parking lot of the school turn left on Henry Street. Go straight on Henry Street for two blocks. Be careful when you cross Montgomery Street. This is a busy intersection. Stay on Henry Street until you get to Grand Street. Next, you will pass Fong's Market on the right and Jones' Restaurant on the left. After that, you should turn left on Grand Street and walk one block to Columbia Avenue. Then, you must turn right on Columbia and walk one more block. Finally, you will see the park on your left.

You should wear sports clothes to the party because we're going to play soccer. Don't bring your lunch. We're going to have sandwiches, drinks, and cake after the soccer game. If it rains, we are going to have the party at the City Recreation Center. The center is next to Downing Playground. Please call us by Friday to let us know that you will come. Our phone number is 555-3032.

See you at the party!
The Lee Family

C **Write captions.** Write a sentence for each picture on page 45. Use sentences from the reading.

1. It is Nathan's birthday and we are going to have a party for him!

2. _____

3. _____

4. _____

5. _____

6. _____

7. _____

8. _____

L. A. T. C. Mission College
3000 Mission College Blvd.
Santa Clara, CA 95054
(408) 855-5095

VOCABULARY

A Find each word in the reading on page 44. Look at the words around it to guess the meaning. Compare your answers with a partner.

Nouns		Verbs	
avenue	market	come	stay (on)
blocks	parking lot	follow	turn (right/left)
directions	playground	get (to)	walk
house	school	be (on the right/left)	go (straight)
intersection	street	pass	

Learn new words. Write them in your personal dictionary.

B Write the word that best completes the sentence.

1. Nathan's friends walked from the _____parking lot_____ to the playground.

2. They had to cross a very busy _____.

3. Next they walked two _____.

4. The party was at a _____, not at Nathan's _____.

5. Nathan's _____ were easy to follow.

6. Everyone from Nathan's class at _____ came to the party.

C Complete the sentences with direction verbs and phrases.

come	~~follow~~	pass	get to
stay on	turn	on the right	walk

1. _____Follow_____ these directions to come to my party.

2. You can _____ or drive to my house from our school.

3. From the school parking lot, _____ right onto Main Street.

4. _____ Main Street for two blocks.

5. You should _____ a market.

6. The market should be _____.

7. After one more block, you should _____ my house.

8. We hope you can _____ to my party.

Imperative Sentences

Simple Present	Imperative (Affirmative)	Imperative (Negative)
You follow the directions. **You turn** right.	**Follow** the directions. **Turn** right.	**Don't follow** the directions. **Don't turn** right.

Imperative sentences are commands. Use them to tell people what to do.

A Write the words in the correct order to make imperative sentences.

1. directions / follow / these <u>Follow these directions.</u>

2. turn left / from the parking lot _____

3. Henry Street / stay on / for two blocks _____

4. past / Fong's Market / walk _____

5. don't / Grand Street / cross / quickly _____

6. don't / clothes / nice / wear _____

7. the City Recreation Center / come / to _____

8. don't / to call/ soon / forget _____

Modal Verbs

Modal Verb	Purpose
You **can** come from Henry School. Then, you **must** turn right on Columbia. You **should** turn left on Grand Street.	ability necessity recommendation

Modals are helping verbs. They help the verb give more information.

B Find five modals in the reading on page 44. Write the complete sentences.

1. <u>You can come from Henry School to the park on foot.</u>

2. _____

3. _____

4. _____

5. _____

C Complete the sentences. Use a modal to show the purpose in parentheses.

1. You _____ should _____ come to my dance class. (recommendation)

2. You _____ walk or drive from your house. (ability)

3. First you _____ turn left onto Grove Street. (necessity)

4. You _____ follow Grove Street for five blocks. (necessity)

5. Finally, you _____ then turn left on Pickering Street. (recommendation)

6. You _____ be careful crossing the street. (recomendation)

7. You _____ come any time between three and five o'clock. (ability)

8. You _____ knock loudly so we can hear you. (necessity)

ORGANIZATION

Sequential Order

A Reorganize the following group of sentences. Number them in the correct sequential order. Use information from the reading on page 44.

> **Remember!**
> Sequential order tells the order in which you should do things. In the reading on page 40, Jennifer gives her guests directions to the party in the order they should walk. You can use sequence words to show sequential order.
>
> First, . . .   Next, . . .   Then, . . .
> After that, . . .   Finally, . . .

_____ Stay on Henry Street until you get to Grand Street.

___1___ Turn left on Henry Street from the parking lot of the school.

_____ You should turn left on Grand Street and walk one block to Columbia Avenue.

_____ You will see the park on your left.

_____ Go straight on Henry Street for two blocks.

B Rewrite the directions. Add sequence words.

First, turn left on Henry Street from the parking lot of the school.

WRITING STRATEGIES

Pronoun Reference

The underlined words refer back to nouns in the sentences. Write the word to which each pronoun refers.

1. It is Maggie's last day of school and we are going to have a party for her. _____Maggie_____

2. The students are planning the party. They are bringing snacks and drinks. _____

3. The teachers have made her a gift. It is a t-shirt with all the students' names. _____

4. The principal is bringing music. She loves to share her CDs. _____

5. Maggie's parents can come to the party. Let's give them directions. _____

6. They should come to the school by bus. It is on the bus route. _____

WRITING CONVENTIONS

Homonyms

Write the correct homonym to complete each sentence. Rewrite the passage with the correct words.

Please come (1) _____to_____ (to/two/too) Victoria's party. (2) _____ (Here/Hear) are the directions from school (3) _____ (two/to/too) her house. Take a left on Fox Street from the school parking lot. Follow Fox Street for (4) _____ (two/to/too) blocks. (5) _____ (Then/Than) you will pass a playground on the left. (6) _____ (There/They're/Their) is also a market on the right. Turn right after the market. This is James Avenue. Stay on James Avenue for three blocks. Our house is number 745 James Avenue. (7) _____ (It's/Its) on the left. We hope you will (8) _____ (accept/except) the invitation and come to the party.

Technical Writing

Technical writing often gives instructions. It sometimes explains how to get to a place. It sometimes explains how to do something. Written directions and recipes are examples of technical writing.

 A **Read.** Read the directions to Avri's party.

http://www.eaton*school*news.ed

Dear Friends,

We are having a party to celebrate the new school year. The party is on October 2, from 3-5 P.M. It is going to be at Carla's Café downtown. We are going to play games, sing, and dance. After that, we are going to eat dinner. Carla's has great food!

Here are the directions from Lake School to Carla's Café. First, turn right on Marconi Drive from the parking lot of the school. Stay on Marconi until the first traffic light, then turn right again. This is Lee Boulevard. Stay on Lee for about three blocks. Turn left at the corner of Lee Boulevard and Main Street. Main is a long street. Stay on it for a mile. At Grand Park, Main Street changes to Canal Street. At that point, you must turn right and then quickly turn left. Be careful here. This intersection is sometimes very busy. You should stay on Canal Street for ten or twelve more blocks. Finally, stop when you get to 3904 Canal Street. This is the café. It is blue and white.

Please call and tell us if you can come to the party by September 15. My phone number is 555-7848. I really hope you can all come!

See you soon.
Avri

Learn new words. Write them in your personal dictionary.

 B **Follow the directions.** Draw a line on the map on page 51 to show the way from Lake School to Avri's party. Then, use the map to complete Miguel's note. Use words and sentences from Avri's directions.

Directions to a Party

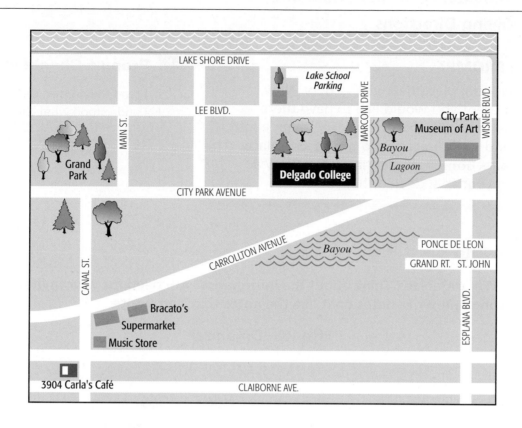

Dear C. J.,

Avri is having a party at Carla's Café. You should come. It's on October 2, from 3-5 P.M. Here's how to get to the party from our school.

See you there!
Your friend,
Miguel

STEP–BY–STEP WRITING

Purpose: Giving Directions

WRITING PROMPT

Think of a special place near your school. Now, think of an event you would like to have there. Write an invitation to your friends. Tell them about the event and give directions to this special place. Give clear directions in sequential order. Draw a map to help your friends find their way.

STEP 1 Pre-write

Look at Avri's *Wh-* organizer. Think about the information you need for your invitation. Copy the drawing and write notes on it like the notes that Avri wrote.

Avri's *Wh-* Organizer

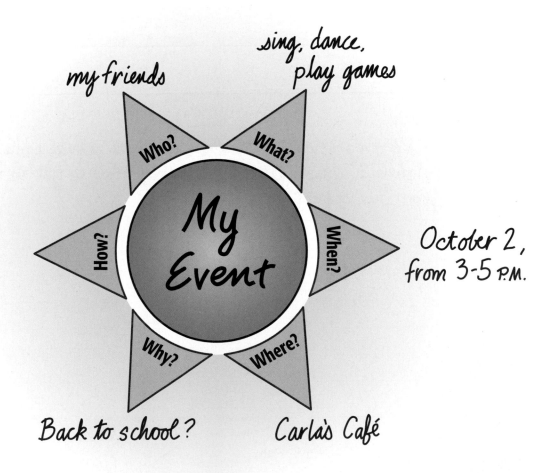

STEP 2 Organize

Look at Avri's sequence organizer. Copy the organizer or make one on a computer.
Add steps if you need to. Complete the organizer with directions to your special place.

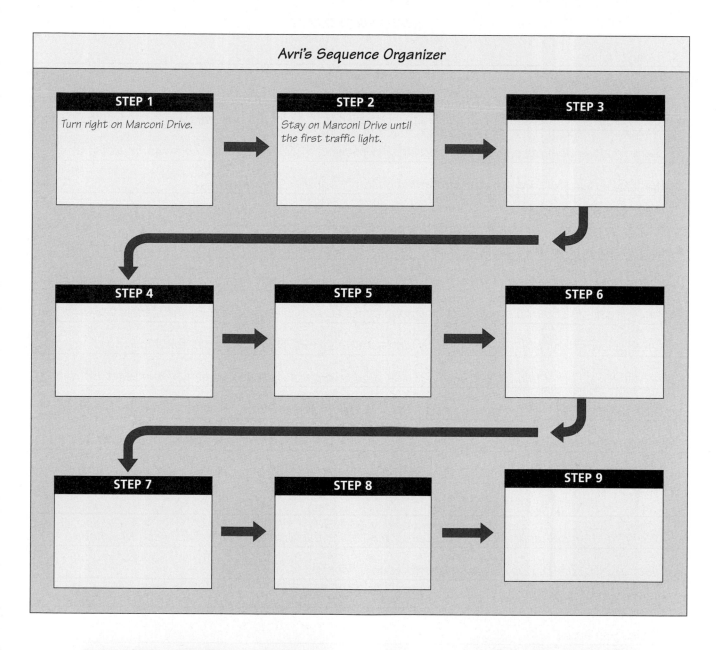

Avri's Sequence Organizer

STEP 1
Turn right on Marconi Drive.

STEP 2
Stay on Marconi Drive until the first traffic light.

STEP 3

STEP 4

STEP 5

STEP 6

STEP 7

STEP 8

STEP 9

STEP 3 Draft and Revise

A **Practice. Look at Avri's first draft. How can she improve it? Answer the questions.**

AVRI'S FIRST DRAFT

(1) Dear Friends,

(2) We are having a party too celebrate the new school year. (3) The party is on October 2, from 3-5 P.M. (4) It is going too be at Carla's Café downtown. (5) We are going to play games, sing and dance. (6) After that, we are going to eat dinner. (7) Carla's has great food!

(8) Here are the directions from Lake School to Carla's Café. (9) From the parking lot of the school, turn right on Marconi Drive. (10) Stay on Marconi until the first traffic light, then turn right again. (11) This is Lee Boulevard. (12) Stay on Lee for about three blocks. (13) Turn left at the corner of Lee Boulevard and Main Street. (14) Main is a long street. (15) Stay on it for a mile.

(16) At Grand Park, Main Street changes to Canal Street. (17) At that point, you must turn right and then quickly turn left. (18) Be careful here. (19) This intersection is sometimes very busy.

(20) You stay on Canal Street for ten or twelve more blocks. (21) Stop when you get to 3904 Canal Street. (22) This is the café. (23) The café is blue and white.

(24) You can call and tell us if you can come to the party by September 15. (25) My phone number is 555-7848. (26) I really hope you can all come!

(27) See you soon.

   Avri

---

1. Which word best replaces the word *too* in sentence 2?

    A at

    Ⓑ to

    C two

    D on

2. Which sequence word should Avri write at the beginning of sentence 9?

    A First,

    B Then,

    C Next,

    D Finally,

3. Which modal would be best in sentence 20?

    A can

    B should

    C are

    D will

4. Which sequence word should Avri write at the beginning of sentence 21?

    A First,

    B Then,

    C After that,

    D Finally

5. How can Avri best rewrite sentence 23 with a pronoun so she doesn't have to use the same words again?

    A The café is blue and white!

    B The café is white and blue.

    C It is blue and white.

    D The café is blue.

6. How can Avri best rewrite sentence 24 to include a polite imperative?

    A Please call and tell us if you can come to the party by September 15.

    B You should call and tell us if you can come to the party.

    C Don't call and tell us if you can come to the party.

    D Call and tell us if you can come to the party.

B **Draft. Write a first draft for your letter. Use your notes from Steps 1 and 2.**

C **Revise. Read your first draft. How can you improve it? Look at the revision checklist. Revise your writing.**

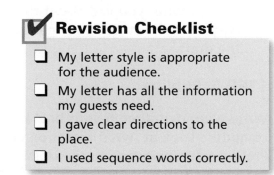

Revision Checklist

- ❑ My letter style is appropriate for the audience.
- ❑ My letter has all the information my guests need.
- ❑ I gave clear directions to the place.
- ❑ I used sequence words correctly.

STEP 4 Edit

A Practice. Look at the sentences. Choose the best word or phrase to complete each sentence.

1. You _____ follow these directions to come to my house.

   A are
   B will
   C have
   (D) should

2. After the bridge, _____ left onto Hastings Street.

   A you are
   B you should
   C turn
   D follow

3. You will pass a market and a playground. After _____ turn right.

   A it
   B her
   C the market and playground
   D these

4. After you pass Tina's Tanning, you _____ turn left.

   A will
   B won't
   C should
   D are

5. _____ park on the street! You could get a ticket.

   A You will
   B Don't
   C You won't
   D You should

6. _____ house is white and black.

   A Their
   B They're
   C There
   D They'll

B Edit. Reread your draft from Step 3. Look at the editing checklist. Edit your writing.

C Peer Edit. Exchange drafts with a partner. Tell your partner what you like about the draft. Look at the editing checklist. Tell your partner how to improve the draft.

STEP 5 Publish

Write your invitation in your best handwriting or use a computer. Look at Avri's invitation on page 50 for ideas. Present your invitation to the class.

✔ **Editing Checklist**

my		
me	partner	
❏	❏	used imperatives and modals correctly.
❏	❏	used pronouns to make my writing more interesting.
❏	❏	used words with the correct spelling and meaning.
❏	❏	used correct spelling, punctuation, and capitalization.

TECHNOLOGY

Using Map Web Sites

Do a **keyword** search for "map Web sites." Enter your school's address into three of the map searches. How are the maps different at each Web site? How are they the same? Print the map if you can. Add it to your invitation.

GROUP WRITING

Work in a group to write a letter about one of these topics. Follow the steps below.

1. Choose a topic.
2. Decide the letter form.
3. Do research if you need to.

4. Write a first draft.
5. Revise and edit the letter with your group.
6. Present your group's letter to the class.

Topic 1

Write a letter to a friend or family member. In the opening paragraph, describe where you are, what you are doing, and how you are feeling right now. Then, look at the picture below. Pretend you were at this basketball game yesterday. In the body paragraph, describe what happened at the game.

Topic 2

Invite a friend or family member to your favorite restaurant for lunch. Give him/her directions from the school (red star) to the restaurant (blue star).

_____

_____

_____

_____

_____

_____

TIMED WRITING

Choose one writing prompt. Complete the writing task in 45 minutes.

WRITING PROMPT 1

Write a letter or e-mail to a friend. Describe what you are doing now, what you did last week, and what you will do next week. Use chronological order to describe these events.

WRITING PROMPT 2

Plan a party for your class. Make an invitation. You can invite one family member. Give him/her information about the event and directions from his/her work to your school.

💡 Test Tip

Remember form! Friendly letters and invitations have **a greeting, a body,** and **a closing.** Remember that the **body** of your letter or invitation can be more than one paragraph long. The **body** should include information about you and questions for the receiver.

SELF–CHECK

Think about your writing skills. Check (✔) the answers that are true.

1. I understand . . .
   - ❑ weather words.
   - ❑ sensory adjectives.
   - ❑ letter writing expressions.
   - ❑ nouns for places.
   - ❑ verb phrases for directions.

2. I can correctly use . . .
   - ❑ the present continuous tense.
   - ❑ the past continuous tense.
   - ❑ statements with *there was* and *there were*.
   - ❑ quantity adjectives.
   - ❑ the imperative form.
   - ❑ the modal verbs *can, should,* and *must*.

3. I can correctly use . . .
   - ❑ prepositions in spatial descriptions.
   - ❑ pronouns to make my writing more interesting.

4. I can correctly use . . .
   - ❑ greetings and closings in a letter.
   - ❑ homonyms.

5. I can organize my writing by . . .
   - ❑ space.
   - ❑ sequence.

6. I can write to . . .
   - ❑ describe an event and feelings.
   - ❑ give directions.

Unit 5

Write a Story

UNIT OBJECTIVES

Writing
personal narrative

Organization
parts of a story

Writing Strategies
cause and effect words

Writing Conventions
reported vs. direct speech

Vocabulary
nouns for work
feelings adjectives

Grammar
complex sentences with *because,*
and *when*
object pronouns

Technology
researching job opportunities

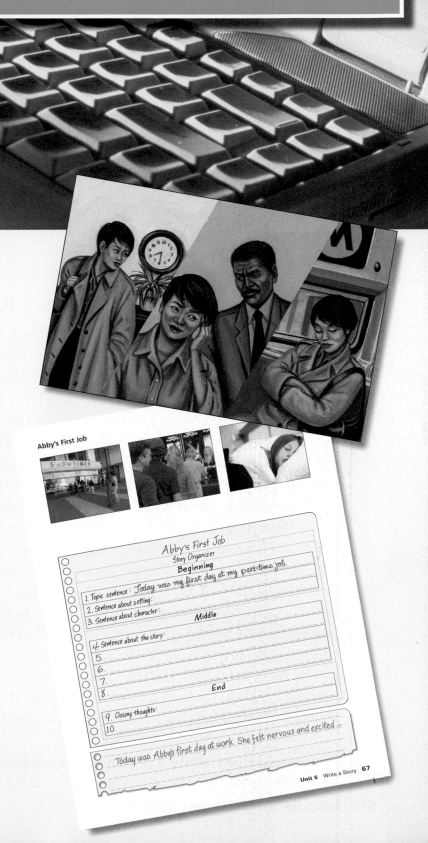

Abby's First Job

Abby's First Job
Story Organizer
Beginning

1. Topic sentence: Today was my first day at my part-time job.
2. Sentence about setting:
3. Sentence about character:
Middle

4. Sentence about the story:
5.
6.
7.
8.
End

9. Closing thoughts:
10.

Today was Abby's first day at work. She felt nervous and excited ...

A **Discuss. Complete the information. Compare answers with a partner.**

1. What was an event that made you happy?

   _____

2. What was an event that made you sad?

   _____

3. What was an event that made you angry?

   _____

4. What was an activity that made you exhausted?

   _____

5. What was an event that made you nervous?

   _____

B **Read. Read the personal narrative.**

Mrs. Lee's Bad Day

Today was not a typical day for Jennifer and Nathan's mother, Mrs. Lee. It was difficult and frustrating. In the morning, she was late for her job as an office assistant. In the afternoon, her boss got angry with her. Now, she is exhausted. Mrs. Lee is happy that most days are different.

At 7:00 A.M., Mrs. Lee got up as usual. She took a shower and made breakfast for the family. After breakfast, she got ready for work. When Jennifer and Nathan went to school at 8:00, Mrs. Lee left for work. She walked to her bus stop and waited and waited. Finally, the bus came, but it was twenty minutes late! Then, on the way downtown, the bus broke down. As a result, everybody got off and waited for another bus. When Mrs. Lee thought about the time, she became really nervous! Finally, she took a taxi to her office because she was very late. When her boss saw her, he wasn't very happy! Mrs. Lee worked hard all morning. However, Mrs. Lee forgot to mail an important letter because she had a bad morning. When her boss found the letter, he was very angry. Mrs. Lee felt terrible, so she had a bad afternoon, too.

Late that evening, Mrs. Lee took the bus home. She was exhausted. When she got home, she told her family about her day. They were very understanding. Her mother said, "Because you are so tired, I'll make dinner. You should relax." Her husband told her that he was sorry she had a bad day. Then, he brought her a cold drink. Jennifer and Nathan even said that they would do the dishes. After dinner, Mrs. Lee felt much better. She thought to herself, "It's good to have a nice family. They can make even a bad day better."

 C **Write captions. Write a sentence for each picture on page 61. Use sentences from the reading.**

1. In the morning, she was late for her job. In the afternoon, her boss got angry with her. Now, she is exhausted.

2. _____
_____
_____

3. _____
_____

4. _____
_____

5. _____
_____

6. _____
_____

7. _____
_____

8. _____
_____

VOCABULARY

A Find each word or phrase in the reading on page 60. Look at the words around it to guess the meaning. Compare your answers with a partner.

Nouns	Verbs	Adjectives	
boss	apologize	angry	frustrating
office	break down	difficult	nervous
assistant	get off	exhausted	understanding
	wait		

Learn new words. Write them in your personal dictionary.

B Complete the sentences with words from the list. Change the verb tenses as needed.

boss	break down	get off	late	assistant	apologize	~~wait~~

1. Mrs. Lee _____waited_____ for the bus.

2. Then, the bus _____!

3. All of the people were angry when they had to _____ the bus.

4. At work, Mrs. Lee's _____ asked about the important letter.

5. Mrs. Lee works hard and is a good _____.

6. Everyone in her _____ likes her.

C Find the adjectives in the reading. Then, write sentences that use them to describe the characters' feelings.

angry	difficult	exhausted	frustrating	~~nervous~~	understanding

1. When Mrs. Lee thought about her work, she became really nervous!

2. _____

3. _____

4. _____

5. _____

6. _____

➤Learn more in the Grammar Reference,
pages 149–164.

Dependent Clause	Independent Clause	Complex Sentence
Because she had to take a taxi, . . .	Mrs. Lee was thirty minutes late.	Because she had to take a taxi, Mrs. Lee was thirty minutes late.
When Mrs. Lee thought about the time, . . .	She became really nervous!	When Mrs. Lee thought about the time, she became really nervous!

Complex sentences are made of two or more **clauses**. A **clause** is a group of words with a subject and a verb.

Independent clauses are complete sentences. **Dependent clauses** are not complete sentences. Writers often join two clauses with words such as *because* and *when*. When the dependent clause is at the beginning of the sentence, use a comma after a dependent clause.

When Mrs. Lee thought about the time, she became really nervous!

A **Find four more complex sentences with *because* or *when* in the reading on page 60. Copy them on the lines below.**

1. When her boss saw her, he wasn't very happy! _____

2. _____

3. _____

4. _____

5. _____

B **Answer the following questions with complex sentences that use *because* or *when*.**

1. Why was Mrs. Lee late for work?

   Mrs. Lee was late for work because the bus broke down. _____

2. When was her boss angry?

   _____

3. Why did Mrs. Lee forget to mail the letter?

   _____

4. When will Mrs. Lee tell her family the whole story of her day?

   _____

5. Why will Mrs. Lee's mother cook dinner?

   _____

Sentence	Subject	Object	Object Pronoun	New Sentence
The boss got angry with Mrs. Lee.	The boss	Mrs. Lee	her	The boss got angry with ~~Mrs. Lee~~ her.
Mrs. Lee forgot to mail the letter.	Mrs. Lee	the letter	it	Mrs. Lee forgot to mail ~~the letter~~ it.

The **subject** of a sentence does something to the **object**.
Pronouns take the place of nouns. They can also be **objects**.
The object pronouns are: *me, you, him, her, it, us,* and *them*.

C Answer the following questions with information from the reading on page 60. Replace the objects with object pronouns.

1. Did Mrs. Lee make breakfast for Nathan and Jennifer?
   Yes, Mrs. Lee made breakfast for them.

2. Did Mrs. Lee take the bus?
   _____

3. When Mrs. Lee came in late, was the boss happy with Mrs. Lee?
   _____

4. Did Mrs. Lee mail the letter?
   _____

5. How did the boss feel about Mrs. Lee?
   _____

6. Who will listen to Mrs. Lee's story?
   _____

WRITING STRATEGIES

Using Cause-and-Effect Words

Fill in the cause-and-effect chart with information from the reading on page 60.

Remember!
An effect is an event that happens as a result of a cause. Use cause-and-effect words to signal that one event is the result of another.
Use commas after the cause-and-effect word or phrase:
As a result,   Then,   Therefore,
Because . . .

Cause	Effect	Signal word
	All of the people got off the bus.	As a result,
	Mrs. Lee forgot to mail an important letter.	

Direct vs. Reported Speech

Find two more examples of reported speech in the reading on page 60. Change the reported speech to direct speech.

1. When she got home, she told her family about her day.

   When she got home she said, "I had a terrible day."

2. _____

   _____

3. _____

   _____

Remember!

Direct speech gives the actual words that a person said. Put quotation marks where the speaker's words start and end. Put a comma between the quotation and the speaker. Direct quotes always begin with a capital letter. Reported speech tells what someone said. Do not use quotation marks with reported speech. The verb form changes in reported speech.

Direct speech	Mrs. Lee said, "I'm sorry."
Reported speech	Mrs. Lee said that she was sorry.

ORGANIZATION

Parts of a Story

Find the beginning, the middle, and the end of the story on page 60. Write two sentences from each part of the story in the chart below.

Remember!

Stories have a beginning, a middle, and an end. The beginning introduces the story and tells about the setting and characters. The middle gives details about the action or plot of the story. The end tells what the story means or why it is important.

Story Organizer
Beginning
1. Today was not a typical day for Jennifer and Nathan's mother, Mrs. Lee.
2. _____
Middle
1. _____
2. _____
End
1. _____
2. _____

DO NOT WRITE IN THIS BOOK

Personal Narrative

A story tells about what happens to characters. Characters are the people in the story. Setting is the time and place of a story. A story has a beginning, a middle, and an end. Personal narrations and creative writing are examples of stories.

 A Read. Read Abby's personal narration.

My First Job

Today was my first day at my part-time job. I woke up early. I stayed in bed for a few minutes. I thought about the day. I thought about the movie theater. I thought about my boss, Mrs. Obar. I was excited and nervous.

At 8:00, I got out of bed. I showered and got dressed in my new uniform. I felt important in the special shirt and pants. Before I went to the kitchen, I put on my nametag. When my mom saw me, she said, "Good morning, theater employee!" My dad told me to hurry up and eat breakfast. At 10:00, my dad dropped me off at the movie theater. When I arrived, Mrs. Obar told me that there wouldn't be many people coming to the movies in the morning. Then, she left me at the entrance. At first, only one or two people came. Then, a few more people came in. And then, it happened. A large bus stopped outside the theater. There were more than forty people on the bus. Slowly they began to get off the bus. They bought their tickets. Then, they came toward me in small groups. Each person had a different question. "Where's the bathroom?" asked one man. "Where's the food?" said another. I got nervous because I didn't know the answers. Finally, the people went in the theaters. I relaxed. Then, a man tapped me on the shoulder. I turned to answer his question and saw that it was my dad! "Are you ready to come home?" he asked. I couldn't believe it! It was already 2:00. I was finished for the day.

My first day of work was a little difficult. I was very nervous because I didn't know very much. Since the people were very nice, it was OK. I asked a lot of questions. In the end, it was fun, but I hope there aren't any more buses.

Learn new words. Write them in your personal dictionary.

 B Label the paragraph. Reread Abby's story. Label the beginning, middle, and end. Find the characters and setting. Label them with the words *characters* and *setting*. Fill in the outline for Abby's story. Use information from her personal narrative. Then, complete the paragraph.

Abby's First Job

Abby's First Job
Story Organizer

Beginning

1. Topic sentence: Today was my first day at my part-time job.

2. Sentence about setting: _____

3. Sentence about character: _____

Middle

4. Sentence about the story: _____

5. _____

6. _____

7. _____

8. _____

L. A. T. C. Mission College
3000 Mission College Blvd.
Santa Clara, CA 95054
(408) 855-5095

End

9. Closing thoughts: _____

10. _____

Today was Abby's first day at work. She felt nervous and excited ...

STEP–BY–STEP WRITING

Purpose: Tell a Story

WRITING PROMPT

Write a three-paragraph personal narrative about an important event in your life. Be sure your narrative has a beginning, a middle, and an end. Tell why the event was important.

STEP 1 Pre-write

Look at Abby's *Wh-* organizer. Think about the details you are going to include in your personal narrative. Make a *Wh-* organizer about your event.

me, my family,
Mrs. Obar,
all the people

Who?

What?

My First Job

When?

first day,
10 A.M.

How?

I felt happy
and important

Why?

Where?

because I
could help people
and I am old
enough to have a job

STEP 2 Organize

Look at Abby's story organizer. Organize your topic sentence, beginning, middle, and end. Copy the story organizer or make one on a computer. Complete the organizer with information about your story.

Topic Sentence	Today was my first day at my part-time job.
Beginning: Setting Characters	I stayed in bed. I thought about the movie theater. I thought about my boss, Mrs. Obar.
Middle: Story	At 10:00, my dad dropped me off at the movie theater. A large bus stopped outside the theater. Then a man tapped me on the shoulder.
End: Conclusion and Importance	My first day of work was a little difficult. I was very nervous because I didn't know very much. Since the people were very nice, it was OK. I asked a lot of questions. In the end, it was fun, but I hope there aren't any more buses.

A Practice. Look at Abby's first draft. How can she improve it? Answer the questions on page 71.

Abby's First Draft
My First Job

(1) Today was my first day at my part-time job. (2) I woke up early. (3) I stayed in bed for a few minutes. (4) I thought about the day. (5) I thought about my boss, Mrs. Obar. (6) I was excited and nervous.

(7) At 8:00, I got out of bed. (8) I showered and got dressed in my new uniform. (9) I felt important in the special shirt and pants. (10) Before I went to the kitchen, I put on my nametag. (11) My mom saw me. (12) She said, "Good morning theater employee!" (13) My dad said, "Hurry up and eat breakfast." (14) At 10:00, my dad dropped me off at the movie theater. (15) When I arrived, Mrs. Obar told me that there wouldn't be many people coming to the movies in the morning. (16) Then, she left me at the entrance. (17) At first, only one or two people came. (18) Then, a few more people came in. (19) And then, it happened. (20) A large bus stopped outside the theater. (21) There were more than forty people on the bus. (22) Slowly they began to get off the bus. (23) They bought their tickets. (24) Then, they came toward me in small groups. (25) Each person had a different question. (26) "Where's the bathroom?" asked one man. (27) "Where's the food?" said another. (28) I got nervous. (29) I didn't know the answers. (30) Finally, the people went in the theater. (31) I relaxed. (32) Then, a man tapped me on the shoulder. (33) I turned to answer his question and saw it was my dad! (34) "Are you ready to come home?" he asked. (35) I couldn't believe it! It was already 2:00. (36) I was finished for the day.

(37) My first day of work was a little difficult. (38) I was very nervous because I didn't know very much (39) Since the people were very nice, it was OK. (40) I asked a lot of questions.

1. Which sentence can Abby add after sentence 4 to best introduce the setting?

   A I like sleeping in my bed.
   B I thought about the movie theater.
   C Movie theaters are exciting places.
   D I always stay in bed and think about my day.

2. How can Abby combine sentences 11 and 12 to make a complex sentence?

   A When my mom saw me, she said, "Good morning, theater employee!"
   B Because my mom saw me, she said, "Good morning, theater employee!"
   C My mom saw me and she said, "Good morning, theater employee!"
   D My mom saw me, she said, "Good morning, theater employee!"

3. How can Abby correctly change sentence 13 from direct speech to reported speech?

   A My dad said hurry up and eat breakfast.
   B My dad told me hurry up and eat breakfast.
   C My dad told me, "Hurry up and eat breakfast."
   D My dad told me to hurry up and eat breakfast.

B **Draft.** Write a first draft for your paragraph. Use your notes from Steps 1 and 2.

C **Revise.** Read your first draft. How can you improve it? Look at the revision checklist. Revise your writing.

4. Which cause and effect signal word can Abby place after sentence 28 to join it to sentence 29 and show the cause and effect relationship?

   A therefore
   B as a result
   C for
   D because

5. Which sentence should Abby add after sentence 40 to best show the importance of the event?

   A In the end, it was fun, but I hope there aren't any more buses.
   B I am happy.
   C I am very tired.
   D I work again next week.

DO NOT WRITE IN THIS BOOK

✔ **Revision Checklist**

   ❏ I have a clear topic sentence.
   ❏ My narrative has a beginning, a middle, and an end.
   ❏ I introduced the setting and the characters.
   ❏ My concluding paragraph tells the importance of the event.

STEP 4 Edit

A **Practice. Look at the sentences. Choose the best substitute for the underlined words. If the sentence is correct, choose "Make no change."**

1. I am <u>happy because</u> I have a job.

   A happy therefore
   B happy, because
   C happy and
   D Make no change.

2. When he goes to <u>work, he</u> takes the bus.

   A work, he
   B work he
   C work, and he
   D Make no change.

3. You were late. <u>Therefore I</u> am upset.

   A Therefore, I
   B Therefore so I
   C Therefore. I
   D Make no change.

4. Brooke and Matt worked hard last week. Their boss gave extra money to <u>her</u>.

   A him
   B it
   C them
   D Make no change.

✔ Editing Checklist

me	my partner	
☐	☐	used cause and effect words correctly
☐	☐	used complex sentences with *because* and *when* correctly
☐	☐	indented paragraphs
☐	☐	correctly punctuated speech with quotation marks and commas
☐	☐	used correct spelling, punctuation, and capitalization

B **Edit. Reread your draft from Step 3. Look at the editing checklist. Edit your writing.**

C **Peer Edit. Exchange drafts with a partner. Tell your partner what you like about the draft. Look at the editing checklist. Tell your partner how to improve the draft.**

STEP 5 Publish

Rewrite your narrative in your best handwriting or on a computer. Look at Abby's narrative on page 66 for ideas. Add a photograph or drawing if you want. Present your narration to the class.

TECHNOLOGY

Researching Job Opportunities

What kind of work would you like to do for a first job? Where would you like to work? Go to an **Internet search engine**. Do a keyword SEARCH for that type of job. For example, type in "movie theater employment opportunities" and your town name. **Click** SEARCH . Click on a hyperlink for a job **Web site**. What types of jobs are available? Do any of them interest you? What would be the first step in getting a job at that place? Share your findings with the class. **Cite your sources. Write down the Web page title, the Web site title, the publication date, the access date, and the URL.**

Unit 6

Make a Written Request

UNIT OBJECTIVES

Writing
writing a formal letter

Organization
order of importance

Writing Strategies
writing a résumé entry

Writing Conventions
writing a formal letter

Vocabulary
verbs for work
adjectives to describe oneself

Grammar
present perfect
indirect requests
direct requests

Technology
researching job/volunteer
positions online

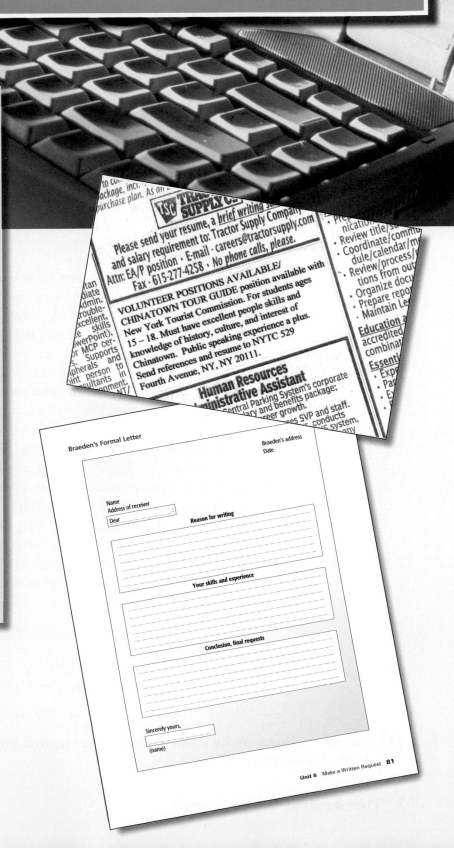

Please send your resume, a *brief writing* and salary requirement to: Tractor Supply Company Attn: EA/P position · E-mail · careers@tractorsupply.com Fax - 615-277-4258 · No phone calls, please.

VOLUNTEER POSITIONS AVAILABLE/
CHINATOWN TOUR GUIDE position available with
New York Tourist Commission. For students ages
15 – 18. Must have excellent people skills and
knowledge of history, culture, and interest of
Chinatown. Public speaking experience a plus.
Send references and resume to NYTC 529
Fourth Avenue, NY, NY 20111.

Braeden's Formal Letter

Braeden's address
Date

Name
Address of receiver
Dear _____ :

Reason for writing

Your skills and experience

Conclusion, final requests

Sincerely yours,

(name)

A **Discuss.** Discuss what the following people do at these jobs. Compare answers with a partner.

1. tour guide
2. baby sitter
3. volunteer
4. camp counselor
5. library aide
6. newspaper delivery person

B **Read.** Read Jennifer's formal letter.

> 1405 Washington Avenue, Apt. #9
> NY, NY 21202
> January 20, 2008
>
> New York Tourist Commission—Chinatown
> 529 Washington Avenue
> NY, NY 21203
>
> Dear Madam/Sir:
>
> I am writing to request an interview for the volunteer position of Chinatown tour guide. I saw your advertisement in Friday's *New York Times*. I am very interested in volunteering for the New York Tourist Commission. I am an active member of the Chinatown community. I know that I would be an excellent tour guide.
>
> I have a lot of experience and skills for the position. I have lived in Chinatown for two years. I have studied about Chinatown's history in school. I have given presentations about Chinatown's restaurants, shopping, and cultural festivals in class. I can speak in front of a group with confidence. These presentations have prepared me to be an excellent Chinatown tour guide. I can speak three languages, too: English, Mandarin, and Cantonese. Also, I am reliable. I never miss work. I have babysat for two years. I have also delivered newspapers this year. I am always prompt and work cheerfully and well. I would be happy to give you a list of references and a résumé of my work experience.
>
> Would you please consider me for the volunteer position of Chinatown tour guide? Chinatown is an important cultural center. I would like to help people get to know my community. I would like to come in for an interview. Please contact me at the above address. Thank you very much.
>
> Sincerely,
>
> *Jennifer Lee*
> Jennifer Lee

C **Write captions.** Write a sentence for each picture on page 75. Use sentences from the reading.

1. I am writing to request an interview for the volunteer position of Chinatown tour guide.

2. _____
_____
_____
_____

3. _____
_____
_____
_____

4. _____
_____
_____
_____

5. _____
_____
_____
_____

6. _____
_____
_____
_____

7. _____
_____
_____
_____

8. _____
_____
_____
_____

9. _____
_____
_____
_____

A Find each word or phrase in the reading on page 74. Look at the words around it to guess the meaning. Compare your answers with a partner.

Nouns		Verbs	Adjectives
advertisement	references	baby sat	prompt
experience	résumé	contact	reliable
interview	skills	delivered	volunteer
position	tour guide	request	
presentations			

Learn new words. Write them in your personal dictionary.

B Complete the following sentences with vocabulary words from the box.

volunteer	~~advertisement~~	skills	reliable	résumé
references	experience	prompt	interview	

1. Jennifer read an _____advertisement_____ about a position at the New York Tourist Commission.

2. The job was an unpaid position as a _____.

3. Jennifer thinks she has the _____ and _____ for the job.

4. When she babysits, she is _____ and _____.

5. She is writing a letter to request an _____.

6. She is happy to send her _____ and _____.

C Answer these questions about yourself.

1. Do you work or volunteer now? If so, where?

2. What is the name of a company or volunteer organization you would like to work for?

3. Why would you like to work there?

4. What skills do you have that would help you work there?

5. What is your work experience?

Indirect and Direct Requests	
Indirect Requests	**Direct Requests**
Would you please send me an application?	*Please send* me an application.

Indirect Requests: *Would* is used to make indirect requests. *Would* is more formal or polite. It is used in formal letters.

Direct Requests: Please + the infinitive is used in polite direct requests.

A Write one direct request for each of the following situations. Use the imperative with *please*. Use *me, to me,* or *for me* in each request. Use the verb in parentheses.

1. You have a question. You need an answer. (answer)

    Please answer a question for me.

2. You need an application form. (send)

3. You want to know the rules. (explain)

4. You need a high school catalog. (send)

5. You want to receive a phone call or letter. (contact)

6. You want to receive a letter at your home address. (write)

B Rewrite each request from Exercise A. Use *Would to* to make an even more polite, indirect request.

1. You have a question. You need an answer. (answer)

    Would you please answer a question for me?

2.

3.

4.

5.

6.

Present Perfect Tense

Present Tense	Past Tense	Present Perfect Tense
I **live** in Chinatown.	I **lived** in Beijing.	I **have lived** in Chinatown for two years.

The present perfect tense uses *has/have* + the past participle to talk about an activity that started in the past and continues until the present.

C Complete the sentences with the present perfect of the verb in parentheses.

1. She _____has worked_____ as a babysitter for over a year. (work)

2. They _____ prompt and reliable. (be)

3. However, she _____ interested in a volunteer tour guide position. (be)

4. I _____ a formal letter. (write)

5. She _____ an interview for the position. (request)

WRITING STRATEGIES

Writing a Résumé Entry

Use the information from Jill's letter on page 79 to list and describe another one of her work experiences. Remember to use strong verbs. Look at an excerpt of Jill's résumé.

Remember!

A résumé is a list and a description of all of your work and education experiences. Résumés also list any awards, hobbies and/or interests. Résumé entries are written in phrases that begin with strong verbs, but have no subject.

Happy Campers Summer Day Camp

Camper, 2005–2008

Camper of the Year Medal, Summer 2007

Attended camp for three years. Learned to swim, canoe, fish, and hike.

Gained thorough knowledge of campgrounds, schedules, and activities.

Name of Company:

_____

Position, time worked there:

_____

Description of duties:

_____

WRITING CONVENTIONS

Writing a Formal Letter

Label the parts of the letter with the correct number:
1 sender's address, 2 receiver's address, 3 date,
4 greeting, 5 body, 6 closing, 7 signature.

Remember!
A formal letter uses formal or polite language. It has both the sender and the receiver's addresses. The formal greeting is followed by a colon(:) It has a formal closing.

355 Canal Street
New Orleans, LA 70119
April 25, 2008

Mrs. Jennifer Westgate
Happy Campers Summer Day Camp
14 Sunshine Lane
New Orleans, LA 70120

Dear Mrs. Westgate:

I am writing to request an interview for the position of Counselor in Training (CIT) at Happy Campers Summer Camp (HCSDC). I read in the spring newsletter that you are looking for CITs. I know I would be excellent for the job.

I have many skills and experience that make me a perfect CIT. I have been a camper at HCSDC for three years now. I am very familiar with the campgrounds, the schedule, and the activities. I love HCSDC. It is my favorite place to be. I even won the Camper of the Year medal last year. At HCSDC, I have learned to swim, canoe, fish, and hike. Now I can teach others. Also, this past year I worked as an aide at Small Tots Daycare Center. The caregivers at the daycare center say I am excellent with children. I play games with them, feed them, and take them outside for walks. I am prompt and hard working.

All of these skills and experiences make me an excellent candidate for the position of CIT. I would be happy to send my résumé and references. Please contact me at the above address. Thank you for your time and consideration.

Sincerely yours,

Jill Sacata
Jill Sacata

L. A. T. C. Mission College
3000 Mission College Blvd.
Santa Clara, CA 95054
(408) 855-5095

ORGANIZATION

Order of Importance

Answer the following questions about the order of Jennifer's letter on page 74.

1. What does Jennifer request in the first paragraph? Why is the other information there?

2. What is the second paragraph about? How does that information connect to the first paragraph? What is the point of the second paragraph?

3. What does Jennifer request in the third paragraph?

4. Of the three paragraphs, which contains the most central point? How important are the other points or requests?

Remember!
Order of importance tells the most important point first, the second point next, and the least important point last. In the reading on page 74, Jennifer first requests an interview because that is most important. She continues, giving her points in order of importance.

Writing a Formal Letter

Formal letters often make requests. They are brief, direct, and limited to one or two points.

A **Read.** Read an excerpt of Braeden Pierson's formal letter.

Learn new words. Write them in your personal dictionary.

3904 Pike Street
Seattle, WA 98102
July 25, 2008

Save the Planet
1 Ecology Way
Seattle, WA 98101

Dear Madam/Sir:

I am writing to request an application to volunteer at Save Our Planet. I am in eighth grade at Davis Middle School. I live in Seattle, about a mile from Save Our Planet headquarters. Last summer, I went to camp at Save Our Planet and loved it. While there, I learned that there are volunteer positions at Save Our Planet for high school students. I would very much like to volunteer at Save Our Planet this summer.

I have a lot of skills and experience that would make me an excellent volunteer at Save Our Planet. I have attended your camp for two summers. I have learned about the Earth and what we can do to save it. This year, science was my best subject in school. I do well in all my classes, but I got an A in science. I did my Science Fair project on the importance of plants. I won an award for my project. Also, I have started an environmentalist club at my school. We began recycling all the classroom and lunchroom paper. We have had two clean-the-campus days. Also this past year, I have volunteered at our library. I am prompt and work well with the librarians.

B **Write a letter.** Copy Braeden Pierson's formal letter into the form. Then, complete his letter, asking Save Our Planet to consider him for the volunteer position and to send him an application. Then, thank them for their time and close the letter formally.

Braeden's Formal Letter

Braeden's address
Date

Name
Address of receiver

Dear _____ :

Reason for writing

Your skills and experience

Conclusion, final requests

Sincerely yours,

_____

(name)

STEP–BY–STEP WRITING

Purpose: Make a Written Request

WRITING PROMPT

Write a three-paragraph letter for a volunteer position or job that interests you. In the opening paragraph, explain why you are writing. In the second paragraph, describe your skills and experience. In the closing paragraph, summarize, make final requests, and thank the person you are writing to.

STEP 1 Pre-write

Look at Braeden's list of skills and work experience. Brainstorm a list of your skills and work experience.

My List of Skills	My List of Work Experience
Science best subject	Attended camp at Save Our Planet for two years
Got an A in science	Started environmental club at school
Did Science Fair project on plants	Began recycling program
Got award for Science Fair project	Worked at library

My List of Skills	My List of Work Experience

STEP 2 Organize

Look at Braeden's letter organizer. Organize your topic, supporting and concluding sentences for each paragraph. Copy the chart or make one on a computer.

Braenden's Letter Organizer	
Introduction Paragraph	I am writing to request an application to volunteer
Topic Sentence	at Save Our Planet.
Supporting Sentence 1	I live in Seattle, about a mile from Save Our Planet headquarters.
Supporting Sentence 2	Last summer, I went to camp at Save Our Planet and loved it.
Supporting Sentence 3	While there, I learned that there are volunteer positions at Save Our Planet for high school students.
Concluding Sentence	I would very much like to volunteer at Save Our Planet this summer.

STEP 3 Draft and Revise

A | **Practice. Look at an excerpt of Braeden's first draft. How can he improve it? Answer the questions.**

(1) 3904 Pike Street

(2) Seattle, WA 98102

(3) Save the Planet

(4) 1 Ecology Way

(5) Seattle, WA 98101

(6) Dear Madam/Sir:

(7) I am in eighth grade at Davis Middle School. (8) I live in Seattle, about a mile from Save Our Planet headquarters. (9) Last summer, I went to camp at Save Our Planet and loved it. (10) While there, I learned that there are volunteer positions at Save Our Planet for high school students. (11) I would very much like to volunteer at Save Our Planet this summer. (12) I am writing to request an application to volunteer at Save Our Planet.

(13) I have attended your camp for two summers. (14) I have learned about the Earth and what we can do to save it. (15) This year, science was my best subject in school. (16) I do well in all my classes, but I got an A in science. (17) I did my science fair project on the importance of plants. (18) I won an award for my project. (19) Also, I have started an environmentalist club at my school. (20) We began recycling all the classroom and lunchroom paper. (21) We have had two clean the campus days. (22) Also this past year, I have volunteered at our library. (23) I am prompt and work well with the librarians.

1. Which information should follow sentence 2?

   A the date
   B the sender's address
   C the receiver's address
   D the greeting

2. Which sentence in paragraph 1 tells the most important point and should be placed first in the paragraph?

   A Sentence 8
   B Sentence 9
   C Sentence 11
   D Sentence 12

3. Which of the following is the best topic sentence for paragraph 2?

   A Save Our Planet Camp is a truly wonderful camp.
   B I have a lot of skills and experience that would make me an excellent volunteer at Save Our Planet.
   C I love studying science both in and out of school.
   D I hope that you will consider me for the position of volunteer at Save Our Planet.

4. Which version of sentence 22 shows that Braeden started volunteering in the past, and still volunteers now?

   A Also this past year, I volunteered at our library.
   B Also this past year, I am volunteering at our library.
   C Also this past year, I have volunteered at our library.
   D Also this past year, I volunteer at our library.

DO NOT WRITE IN THIS BOOK

B **Draft. Write a first draft for your letter. Use your notes from Steps 1 and 2.**

C **Revise. Read your first draft. How can you improve it? Look at the revision checklist. Revise your writing.**

✓ **Revision Checklist**

- ❏ I used proper formal letter conventions such as the sender's address, date, receiver's address, greeting followed by a colon.
- ❏ I used order of importance to organize my letter.
- ❏ I have topic sentences for all my paragraphs.
- ❏ My supporting sentences all relate to the topic sentences.
- ❏ I included a thank you at the end of my letter.

STEP 4 Edit

A Practice. Look at the sentences. Choose the best word or phrase to complete each sentence.

1. I _____ like to request an interview.

   A want
   Ⓑ would
   C must
   D please

2. _____ contact me at the above address.

   A You
   B Can
   C We
   D Please

3. Would you please answer a question _____?

   A by me
   B to me
   C for me
   D at me

4. Dear Sir/Madam _____

   A ,
   B :
   C ;
   D .

5. I _____ at a hospital for the past two years.

   A am volunteering
   B volunteer
   C will volunteer
   D have volunteered

6. 89 Fox Run Road Ipswich _____

   A MA 01936
   B , MA 01936
   C , MA, 01936
   D MA, 01936

B Edit. Reread your draft from Step 3. Look at the editing checklist. Edit your writing.

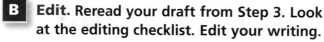 **C** Peer Edit. Exchange drafts with a partner. Tell your partner what you like about the draft. Look at the editing checklist. Tell your partner how to improve the draft.

STEP 5 Publish

Rewrite your letter in your best handwriting or on a computer. Look at Braeden's letter on page 80 for ideas. Present your letter to the class.

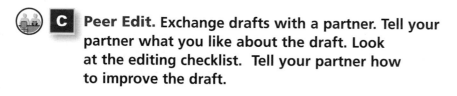

Editing Checklist

me	my partner	
☐	☐	used formal language and the modal *would* correctly
☐	☐	used business writing conventions correctly
☐	☐	used correct spelling, punctuation, and capitalization

TECHNOLOGY

Using an Online Database to Find a Job or Volunteer Position

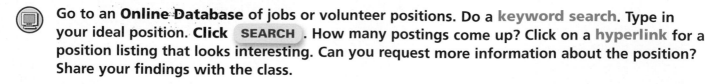 Go to an **Online Database** of jobs or volunteer positions. Do a keyword search. Type in your ideal position. **Click** (SEARCH). How many postings come up? Click on a hyperlink for a position listing that looks interesting. Can you request more information about the position? Share your findings with the class.

GROUP WRITING

Work in pairs to write about one of these topics. Follow the steps below.

1. Choose a topic.
2. Decide the form.
3. Do research if you need to.
4. Write a first draft.
5. Revise and edit the writing with your group.
6. Present your writing to the class.

Topic 1

Think of a time when you were embarrassed or scared. Write about what happened, how you felt, and why.

Topic 2

Write a letter to a company explaining why you are dissatisfied with one of their products. In the body of the letter, tell a story that shows your dissatisfaction. Make a polite request that the company fix the problem.

L. A. T. C. Mission College
3000 Mission College Blvd.
Santa Clara, CA 95054
(408) 855-5095

TIMED WRITING

Choose one writing prompt. Complete the writing task in 45 minutes.

WRITING PROMPT 1

Think of a time you felt proud or important. Tell the story of that event. What happened? How did you feel? Why?

Test Tip

Remember planning!
Remember to brainstorm and organize your ideas into a graphic organizer like a chart or web before beginning your draft.

WRITING PROMPT 2

Write a letter to a company explaining why you are satisfied with one of their products. In the body of the letter, tell a story that shows your satisfaction. Make a request that the company make more products like the one you like.

SELF-CHECK

Think about your writing skills. Check (✔) the answers that are true.

1. I understand . . .
   - ❏ verbs for work.
   - ❏ feelings adjectives.
   - ❏ job phrases.
   - ❏ adjectives to describe oneself.
   - ❏ time expressions.

2. I can correctly use . . .
   - ❏ complex sentences with *because* and *when*.
   - ❏ object pronouns.
   - ❏ the present perfect tense.
   - ❏ indirect requests.
   - ❏ direct requests.

3. I can correctly use . . .
   - ❏ cause and effect words.
   - ❏ a formal letter form.

4. I can correctly use . . .
   - ❏ reported vs. direct speech.
   - ❏ life experiences to write a résumé entry.

5. I can organize my writing by . . .
   - ❏ the beginning, middle, and end.
   - ❏ order of importance.

6. I can write to . . .
   - ❏ tell a story.
   - ❏ make a written request.

Unit 7

Compare and Contrast

1. I moved here over two years ago, but I am still getting used to the changes.
2. _____
3. _____
4. _____
5. _____
6. _____
7. _____
8. _____
9. _____
10. _____

A **Discuss. Work with a partner to make a list of five events that changed your life.**

B **Read. Read Jennifer's compare and contrast essay.**

The event that has changed my life the most is moving to the United States. I moved here over two years ago, but I am still getting used to the changes in my community, my home, my food, and even in me. There are some similarities between my life in China and my life now in the United States, but there are many more differences.

In China, I used to live in a big city called Beijing. It is a busy, crowded, and exciting city. In Beijing, most people drive cars. The traffic is horrible! Once my dad was waiting in traffic for seven hours! Also, in Beijing most families live together. We used to live in a small apartment with my grandparents. My cousins, aunts, and uncles lived down the street. We were always having parties together. The food we ate was really special. We used to eat rice with every meal. We also ate soup for breakfast. I went to school every day, even on weekends. I wore a uniform. I sat at a bench with another girl. There were many more boys than girls in my class. On weekends, my friends and I went to cram school. At this school we studied for the test we had to take to enter junior or senior high school. I was preparing for the senior high school entrance exam when my parents told us we were moving to the States. I was glad I wasn't going to have to take that difficult test! I used to have many friends and family always around me. I miss them now living in the United States.

Although there are many things I miss about my life in Beijing, there are many more things I love about my life in New York City. Like Beijing, New York City is busy, crowded, and exciting. However, most people travel in buses and trains so the traffic isn't as bad. When we first moved here, my dad heard people complain about traffic in New York. My dad laughed to himself. He was remembering the traffic jams in Beijing! Here we live alone in our apartment. I miss having my grandparents and cousins around. On the other hand, I do like having my own bedroom in New York City. I don't have to share whereas I did in Beijing. In contrast to my life in Beijing, I have time to rest and play on the weekends. When we first moved here, my brother and I were sleeping until 11 A.M. every Saturday morning! Also, I have learned to play soccer and the piano because I don't have to spend all my free time studying for entrance exams. We still often eat rice and soup, yet now my family eats American food, too. I always had family and friends around before. Now I write them letters telling them about my different, but wonderful new life.

  C **Write captions. Write a sentence for each picture on page 91. Use sentences from the reading.**

1. I moved here over two
   years ago, but I am still
   getting used to the changes.

2. _____
   _____
   _____

3. _____
   _____

4. _____
   _____
   _____

5. _____
   _____

6. _____
   _____
   _____

7. _____
   _____

8. _____
   _____

9. _____
   _____

10. _____
    _____
    _____

VOCABULARY

A Find each word or phrase in the reading on page 90. Look at the words around it to guess the meaning. Compare your answers with a partner.

Nouns		Verbs	Adjectives	
change	exam	change	crowded	junior
difference	similarity	move	entrance	senior
event	traffic		horrible	

Learn new words. Write them in your personal dictionary.

B Use new vocabulary words to complete the sentences about the event that changed Jennifer's life. Use the information from the reading on page 90.

1. The _____event_____ that has changed Jennifer's life is moving to the United States.

2. She is still getting used to the _____ in her life.

3. There are many _____ between Beijing and New York.

4. One similarity is that both cities are _____ and exciting.

5. One difference is that most people in Beijing drive, so the _____ is bad.

6. In Beijing, Jennifer went to school on the weekends to study for an _____
   _____.

C In the diagram, list the similarities and differences between Jennifer's life in Beijing and New York City.

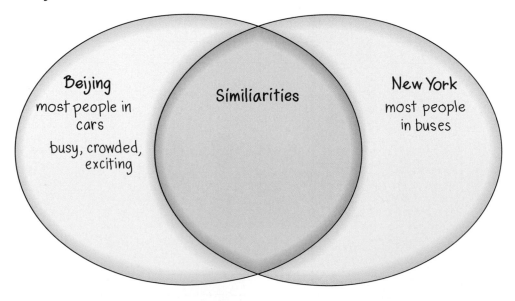

Beijing
most people in cars

busy, crowded, exciting

Similiarities

New York
most people in buses

➤ Learn more in the Grammar Reference, pages 149–164.

Review of Simple Past vs. Past Continuous

Simple Past	Past Continuous
My cousins, aunts, and uncles **lived** down the street.	We **were** always **having** parties together.
I **went** to school every day, even on weekends.	I never missed school unless I **wasn't feeling** well.
At this school we **studied** for the test we **had** to take to enter junior or senior high school.	I **was preparing** for the high school entrance exam when my parents told us we **were moving** to the States.

The **simple past** is used to talk about completed actions in the past.
The **past continuous** is used to talk about an action that took place over a period of time in the past. It is also used to talk about an action that was in progress in the past and was interrupted by past events. Use *while, when,* and *as* to join the sentences. The longer action is in the past.

While I was living in Beijing, I was happy.

A **Complete the sentences with the correct form of the verbs.**

1. While Max ____was resting____, we ____played____ soccer. (rest, play)

2. We _____ in traffic for three hours while we _____ to get to the mall. (wait, try)

3. While Roberto _____, Bruno _____ at a magazine. (studied, look)

4. While Matt and Brooke _____ lunch, the phone _____. (eat, ring)

5. It _____ every day while we _____ our cousins. (rain, visit)

6. When they _____ at the party the lights _____. (dancing, go out)

7. When they _____, their uncles _____ them a gift. (pack, give)

8. While they _____ to some music, their friends _____ to the house. (listen, come)

9. The rain _____ as they _____ to the airport. (stop, go)

Used to	
Verb	**Example**
used to + live *used to* + eat *used to* + have	I **used to live** in a big city called Beijing. In Beijing we **used to eat** rice with every meal. I **used to have** many friends and family always around me.

Use *used to* + the infinitive to talk about habits or routines that happened frequently in the past but that are no longer done.

B Change these past sentences to *used to* + infinitive.

1. My dad was waiting in traffic for seven hours!
   My dad used to wait in traffic for seven hours.

2. My cousins, aunts, and uncles lived down the street.
   _____

3. We were always having parties together.
   _____

4. I went to school every day, even on weekends.
   _____

5. I wore a uniform.
   _____

6. I sat at a bench with another girl.
   _____

ORGANIZATION

Three Paragraph Essay with Thesis Statement

Reread Jennifer's compare and contrast essay on page 90. Answer the following questions.

1. What is the topic sentence in the first paragraph?
   _____

2. What is the thesis statement for the essay?
   _____

3. What is the topic sentence in the second paragraph?
   _____

4. What is the conclusion sentence?
   _____

Remember!
A topic sentence begins a paragraph and introduces the main idea of that paragraph. A thesis statement is a sentence at the end of the introduction paragraph that tells the main points of an essay. In a compare and contrast essay, the thesis statement tells what two things are being compared and contrasted.

WRITING STRATEGIES

Compare and Contrast Signal Words

Reread Jennifer's compare and contrast essay on page 90.
Write sentences that use compare and contrast words.

Comparison Words

1. Like Beijing, New York City is busy, crowded, and exciting.

2. _____

3. _____

Contrast Words

1. _____

2. _____

3. _____

WRITING CONVENTIONS

Verb Agreement

**Fill in the correct form of the verb in parentheses
to complete the sentence.**

1. I _____think/thought_____ studying karate will really
change my life. (think)

2. I _____ shy and nervous around people. (be)

3. I _____ no hand-to-eye coordination. (have)

4. Before the class started, I _____ feeling scared. (be)

5. My karate teacher _____ I will become more confident. (say)

6. She _____ that I will learn the skills I need to succeed. (promise)

7. The other students in the class _____ so strong and confident. (seem)

8. I _____ hoping I would feel more confident by now. (be)

Compare and Contrast Writing

Compare and contrast essays are usually three paragraphs long. The introduction paragraph, introduces the topic. The other two paragraphs describe the two topics and how they are similar and different to each other.

Learn new words. Write them in your personal dictionary.

  A **Read.** Read Karen's compare and contrast essay.

My Life Before and After Karate

Studying karate has really changed my life. When my mother suggested I sign up for a class, I was feeling very nervous. I didn't like sports. I didn't like new experiences. I just wanted to keep my life the same. I was thinking only of the changes that would come with starting karate. I never knew that my life before karate would have some similarities and differences to my life after karate.

Before karate, I used to be shy, nervous, and out-of-shape. At school, I was often alone. I ate lunch with one or two people, but I had no real friends. On the weekends, I used to spend a lot of time alone. I liked to play on the computer, play video games, and practice the piano. Concentration and hand-to-eye coordination were two of my greatest skills. However, I didn't like to show these skills to others. I didn't mind if my sister or my parents heard me play the piano or saw the computer games I created. But I wouldn't share them with others. I even refused to go to my piano recitals. My parents were getting worried about me. I was so shy before I began studying karate!

Then, I went to my first karate class. Many parts of my life changed, but some stayed the same. When we arrived, I was feeling so nervous that I almost didn't get out of the car. My mom talked to me to calm me. So finally, I went in the building. Since that day, I have changed so much. Karate has taught me to be strong in my mind and my body. I am now more confident. Whereas before I didn't have the courage to speak to my classmates, now I do. Now I eat lunch and talk with friends. On the weekends, I still play on the computer, but I also go out with friends. I even performed in a piano recital last weekend. While I was walking up to the piano, I was nervous, but I sat down and played. I was proud of myself for playing in front of others. Similarly to piano and computer games, karate requires concentration and good hand-to-eye coordination. However, unlike these activities, karate is a group sport. It has changed my life in so many wonderful ways.

  B **Write words.** Fill in the diagram with the similarities and differences between Karen's life before karate and her life after. Use information from her essay.

My Life Before and After Karate

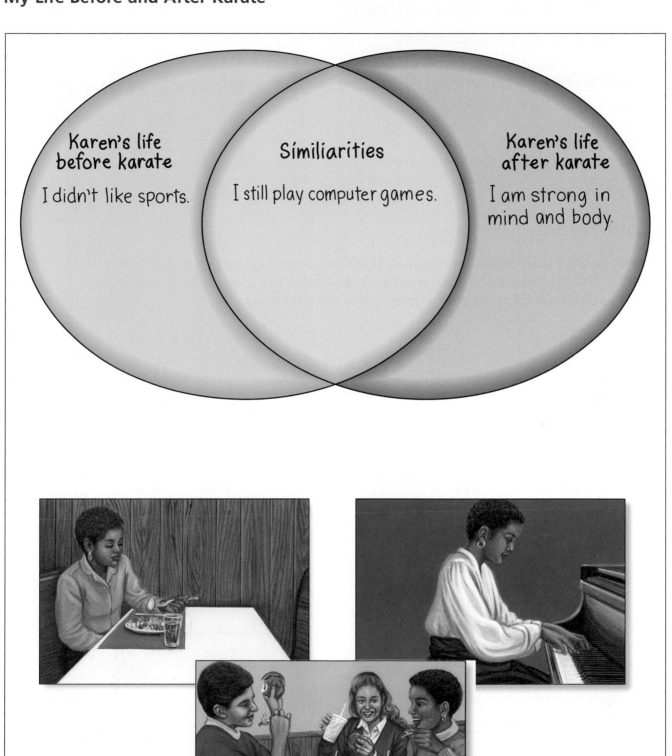

Karen's life
before karate

I didn't like sports.

Similiarities

I still play computer games.

Karen's life
after karate

I am strong in
mind and body.

Purpose: Compare and Contrast

WRITING PROMPT

Write a three-paragraph essay about an event that has changed your life. In the introduction paragraph, introduce your topic. In the other two paragraphs, describe how you were before the event and how you are after the event.

✔ **Prompt Checklist**

☐ I read the prompt carefully.
☐ I understood what the prompt asks me to do.

STEP 1 Pre-write

Look at Karen's three-column organizer. Think about the similarities and differences between her life before and after the event. Complete the three-column organizer below with information for your compare and contrast essay.

Aspects of my life	Before	After
My feelings about sports	Didn't like	Love karate
My personality	Shy, nervous	Confident, strong, social
My activities	Computer, piano—alone	Computer, piano, karate—in a group

Aspects of my life	Before	After

STEP 2 Organize

Look at Karen's paragraph organizer. Organize your essay with topic, supporting, and concluding sentences. Copy the chart or make one on a computer.

Thesis Statement	I never knew that my life before karate would have some similarities and differences to my life after karate.
Topic Sentence in Paragraph 2	Before karate, I was shy, nervous, and out-of-shape.
Supporting Sentence 1	At school, I was often alone. I ate lunch with one or two people, but I had no real friends.
Supporting Sentence 2	On the weekends, I used to spend a lot of time alone.
Concluding Sentence	I was so shy before I began studying karate!

A **Practice. Look at Karen's first draft. How can she improve it? Answer the questions.**

Karen's First Draft
My Life Before and After Karate

(1) Studying karate has really changed my life. (2) When my mother suggested I sign up for a class, I was feeling very nervous. (3) I didn't like sports, (4) I didn't like new experiences. (5) I just wanted to keep my life the same. (6) I was thinking only of the changes that would come with starting karate. (7) I never knew that my life before karate would have some similarities and differences to my life after karate.

(8) Before karate, I was shy, nervous, and out-of-shape. (9) At school, I was often alone. (10) I ate lunch with one or two people, but I had no real friends. (11) On the weekends, I used to spend a lot of time alone. (12) I liked to play on the computer, play video games, and practice the piano. (13) Concentration and hand-to-eye coordination were two of my greatest skills. (14) However, I didn't like to show these skills to others. (15) I didn't mind if my sister or my parents heard me play the piano or saw the computer games I created. (16) I wouldn't share them with others. (17) I even refused to go to my piano recitals. (18) My parents were getting worried about me. (19) I was so shy before I began studying karate!

(20) Then, I went to my first karate class. (21) Many parts of my life changed, but some stayed the same. (22) When we arrived, I was feeling so nervous that I almost didn't get out of the car. (23) Mom talked to me to calm me. (24) So finally, I went in the building. (25) Since that day, I have changed so much. (26) Karate has taught me to be strong in my mind and my body. (27) I am now more confident. (28) Whereas before, I didn't have the courage to speak to my classmates, now I do. (29) Now I eat lunch and talk with friends. (30) On the weekends, I still play on the computer, but I also go out with friends. (31) I even performed in a piano recital last weekend. (32) While I walked up to the piano, I was nervous, but I sat down and played. (33) I was proud of myself for playing in front of others. (34) Similarly to piano and computer games, karate requires concentration and good hand-to-eye coordination. (35) However, unlike these activities, karate is a group sport. (36) It have changed my life in so many wonderful ways.

---

1. Which sentence would best replace sentence 8 to show that Karen's feelings were frequent in the past?

   A Before karate, I am shy, nervous, and out-of-shape.

   B Before karate, I was being shy, nervous, and out-of-shape.

   C Before karate, I used to be shy, nervous, and out-of-shape.

   D Before karate, I felt shy, nervous, and out-of-shape.

2. Which contrast signal word could best be placed at the beginning of sentence 16?

   A Whereas

   B In contrast

   C But

   D On the other hand

3. How can sentence 31 best be changed to show that Karen's walking started first and was interrupted by her feelings?

   A While I am walking up to the piano, I was nervous,

   B While I was walking up to the piano, I was nervous,

   C While I walk up to the piano, I was nervous,

   D While I walked up to the piano, I am nervous,

4. How can Karen best change the verb to agree with the subject in sentence 36?

   A Karate have changed my life in so many wonderful ways.

   B It has changed my life in so many wonderful ways.

   C It have changing my life in so many wonderful ways.

   D It have change my life in so many wonderful ways.

B **Draft. Write a first draft for your essay. Use your notes from Steps 1 and 2.**

C **Revise. Read your first draft. How can you improve it? Look at the revision checklist. Revise your writing.**

✔ Revision Checklist

- ❏ I included information about my life before the event and after the event.
- ❏ I used compare and contrast signal words to show similarities and differences between both times in my life.
- ❏ I included a thesis sentence in my introduction paragraph.
- ❏ My supporting sentences all relate to the topic sentences of my two body paragraphs.
- ❏ My concluding sentence clearly ends my paragraph.

STEP 4 Edit

A Practice. Look at the sentences. Choose the best substitute for the underlined words. If the sentence is correct, choose "Make no change."

1. My family <u>visits</u> my grandparents in Mexico every year.

   A visit
   B are visiting
   C were visiting
   D Make no change.

2. There <u>is</u> many people at the airport today.

   A was
   B are
   C has been
   D Make no change.

3. While it <u>is snowing</u>, the children were outside.

   A snows
   B are snowing
   C was snowing
   D Make no change.

4. My cousins <u>use to study</u> karate.

   A used to study
   B use to studying
   C used study
   D Make no change.

B Edit. Reread your draft from Step 3. Look at the editing checklist. Edit your writing.

C Peer Edit. Exchange drafts with a partner. Tell your partner what you like about the draft. Look at the editing checklist. Tell your partner how to improve the draft.

STEP 5 Publish

Rewrite your essay in your best handwriting or on a computer. Look at Karen's essay on page 96 for ideas. Add a photograph or drawing if you want. Present your essay to the class.

✔ Editing Checklist

me	my partner	
☐	☐	used compare and contrast signal words and change/experience words correctly
☐	☐	used simple past, past continuous, and *used to* correctly
☐	☐	used correct spelling, punctuation, and capitalization

TECHNOLOGY

Researching Historic Events Online

 Go to an Internet search engine. Do a **keyword search**. In quotes, type in your favorite historic event. Click SEARCH . Click on a <u>hyperlink</u> for a reliable .gov, .org, or .com Web site. Discuss with your teacher how to evaluate the reliability of Web sites. Conduct research on at least three Web sites. Then, present to the class how the world is similar and different now after the historic event you researched. Cite your sources. Write down the Web page title, the Web site title, the publication date, the access date, and the URL.

Unit 8

Explain a Topic

UNIT OBJECTIVES

Writing
write a research report

Organization
three-paragraph expository
report

Writing Strategies
supporting facts with evidence

Writing Conventions
paraphrasing vs. quotations

Vocabulary
environmental words

Grammar
if clauses
relative clauses with
who or *that*

Technology
researching sources online

Abdul's Research Report on Endangered Plant

A **Discuss.** Work with a partner. Read the sentences below. Say why you agree or disagree.

1. Animals are important to our world.

2. Plants are important to our world.

 B **Read.** Read Jennifer's research report.

Why the Florida Panther Is Endangered

Why is the Florida panther endangered? The Florida panther, also known as puma, cougar, or mountain lion, lives throughout the Americas. However, it has become endangered in the southern states of the U.S. (Kid's Planet, Puma). According to the scientist team known as the Silversteins, Florida panthers lived all over the southeastern United States before Europeans settled there (Silverstein, 6). There are three main reasons the Florida panther is endangered. People build on panthers' land, hunt their food, or kill them.

People endanger the Florida panther by destroying their habitat. For example, people cut down forests to make space and wood. Panthers who lived in those forests must move to new places. If their new habitats are dangerous, then more panthers will die. The second reason Florida panthers are endangered is because people hunt their food. The Silversteins state that people hunt deer that are "the panthers' favorite food" (Silverstein, 6). If people kill too many deer, then more panthers will die. The third main reason the Florida panther is endangered is that people hunt them. People hunt panthers for sport or protection. For instance, some people hunt panthers because they are afraid they will attack them or their cows.

Not all people threaten Florida panthers. People who are concerned about panthers and other endangered animals work to pass laws, educate others, and save animals. Passing laws that forbid hunting and habitat destruction is one way to help endangered animals. To illustrate, in 1973, the U.S. Fish and Wildlife Service (FWS) passed the Endangered Species Act, a law that forbids hunting or selling of any endangered animals (FWS, Home). Also, local state and town governments pass laws to protect animals. For example, in 1958, the state of Florida prohibited hunting of panthers at any time (Silverstein, 7). People around the world are working to protect endangered animals, like the Florida panther, from becoming extinct. We can help by leaving all wild animals alone and teaching others about endangered animals. We can help endangered animals survive.

Sources:
Puma. Kid's Planet. http://www.kidsplanet.org/factsheets/puma.html.
Endangered Species Act. Fish and Wildlife Service. http://www.fws.gov.
Silverstein, Alvin and Virginia. The Florida Panther. Brookfield: The Millbrook Press, Inc., 1997.

 C **Write captions.** Write a sentence for each picture on page 105. Use sentences from the reading.

1. <u>Why is the Florida panther endangered?</u>

2. _____

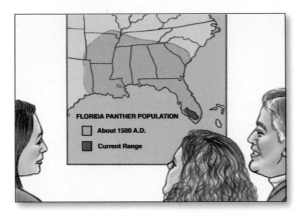

3. _____

4. _____

5. _____

6. _____

7. _____

8. _____

VOCABULARY

A Find each word in the reading on page 104. Look at the words around it to guess its meaning. Compare your answers with a partner.

Nouns	Verbs	Adjectives
actions	destroy	concerned
destruction	prohibit	dangerous
efforts	hunt	endangered
habitat	protect	extinct
species	survive	wild
sport	threaten	

Learn new words. Write them in your personal dictionary.

B Choose the correct words from the box below to complete the sentences. Change the words if necessary.

deer	habitat	prohibit	hunt	survive
protect	concerned	~~endangered~~	extinct	

1. Florida panthers are _____endangered_____ because some people destroy them, their food, or their homes.

2. Panthers' favorite food is _____.

3. Some people ruin panthers' homes or _____.

4. Other people _____ panthers' for sport or protection.

5. Many people are _____ about _____ animals and work hard to help them _____.

6. They pass laws that _____ hunting or selling endangered animals.

7. If we don't work to _____ endangered animals, they may become _____.

C Write six complete sentences about endangered animals, using one or more vocabulary words.

1. _Because of people's efforts, bald eagles are no longer endangered._____

2. _____

3. _____

4. _____

5. _____

6. _____

Complex Sentences with *if* clauses

Dependent clause (Condition)	Independent clause (Result)
If people destroy habitats,	more panthers will become endangered.
If we do not help,	Florida panthers will not survive.

Complex sentences have two kinds of clauses. An **independent clause** is a complete sentence. A **dependent clause** is not a complete sentence.

Use *if* clauses to talk about a possible situation and show what you think will happen.

A   **Read the following sentences. Circle the condition or *if* clause and underline the result.**

1. (If many people work to pass laws and make other efforts,) endangered animals will be protected.

2. If more state and town governments pass laws to protect animals, more animals will remain off the endangered list.

3. Endangered animals can recover if laws stop hunting and limit habitat destruction.

4. You and I can help if we really want to.

5. If we try, we can leave all wild animals alone and teach others about endangered animals.

Relative Clauses with *who* and *that*

Relative clauses with *who*	Relative clauses with *that*
People **who** are concerned about endangered animals work to pass laws.	People hunt deer **that** are the panthers' favorite food.

Relative clauses tell more about a noun in a sentence.

B   **Circle the relative clause in each sentence. What does each clause describe, a person, an animal, or a thing?**

1. People (who cut down forests in Florida) threaten panthers.

2. Panthers that live in Florida are endangered.

3. Deer that live in Florida are panthers' food.

4. People who hunt animals like danger.

5. My friends who like animals plan to start an endangered animals club.

Three-Paragraph Research Report

Research reports can be organized in a three-paragraph essay. The first paragraph introduces the topic and gives the thesis or statement of the three main ideas. The body paragraph explains and gives evidence for the three main ideas. The third paragraph summarizes the main ideas and may tell how the reader can get involved in the subject.

Reread the report on page 104. Complete the outline with the topic sentences and evidence from Jennifer's research report.

Introduction paragraph: Topic sentence	1. Why is the Florida panther endangered?
Thesis statement:	2. _____
Body paragraph: Topic sentence:	3. _____
Main idea 1:	4. People endanger the Florida panther by destroying their habitat.
Supporting evidence for idea 1:	5. For example, people cut down forests.
	6. _____
Main idea 2:	7. _____
Supporting evidence for idea 2:	8. The Silversteins state that, people hunt deer that are "the panthers' favorite food."
	9. _____
Main idea 3:	10. _____
Supporting evidence for idea 3:	11. _____
	12. _____
Conclusion paragraph: Topic sentence:	13. People who are concerned about endangered animals work to pass laws, educate others, and save animals.
Supporting evidence for conclusion paragraph:	14. Passing laws that forbid hunting and habitat destruction is one way to help endangered animals.
	15. _____

WRITING STRATEGIES

Supporting Facts with Evidence

Facts are true statements about a subject. Facts must be supported with **evidence**. Evidence is information that proves something is true. Use **example phrases** to tell that evidence is being given. Some common example phrases are:

such as	including	for instance	like	to illustrate	for example

Reread the report on page 104. Write sentences that include the following example phrases.

1. (for instance) _____

2. (to illustrate) _____

3. (for example) _____

4. (like) _____

WRITING CONVENTIONS

Paraphrasing vs. Quotations

In research reports you can **paraphrase** or **summarize** what a source says or **quote** it directly. Either way, be sure to list the page number or name in parentheses after the paraphrase or quote. Remember to place quotation marks around direct quotes.

Skim Jennifer's research report. Label the following as *paraphrase* or *quotation*. Then, write the name of the book or Web site Jennifer used to find the evidence.

1. According to the scientist team known as the Silversteins, Florida panthers lived all over the southeastern United States before Europeans settled there (6).

    _____paraphrase_____   _____The Florida Panther_____

2. The Silversteins state that people hunt deer that are "the panthers' favorite food" (6).

    _____   _____

3. To illustrate, in 1973, the U.S. Fish and Wildlife Service (FWS) passed the Endangered Species Act, a law that forbids hunting or selling of any endangered animals (FWS, Home).

    _____   _____

4. For example, in 1958, the state of Florida prohibited any hunting of panthers at any time.

    _____   _____

Write a Research Report

Research reports **give facts and information about a topic. Writers do research, take notes, organize their ideas, and write drafts about their topics.**

 A **Read.** Read Abdul's research report about endangered plants.

Why the Cumberland Rosemary Is Important

You have heard of endangered animals. Did you know that plants are endangered too? According to the U.S. Fish and Wildlife Service (FWS) Web site, there are nearly 750 endangered plants in North America. There are three main reasons that animals and people need endangered plants. Plants like the Cumberland rosemary help feed people and animals, help clean the air, and act as important parts of the North American environment.

Some of the endangered plants of North America are important to animals and people as food or medicine. For instance, according to FWS, some birds and insects depend on Cumberland rosemary for food and habitat. People also use rosemary as a spice. Another reason it is important is that it helps clean the air. Like most plants, Cumberland rosemary takes in carbon dioxide in the air. Then, it gives off oxygen that people and animals breathe. If plants like the Cumberland rosemary die out, then harmful gasses will build up in the air (Encyclopedia Americana, 803). The third reason Cumberland rosemary is important is that it is part of our ecosystem. For example, Cumberland rosemary grows on the banks of rivers in Tennessee and Kentucky. There it helps stop floods. If there is a flood, Cumberland rosemary's roots will help stop the dirt from moving. Floods that are dangerous, hurt animals, people, and property.

Too many plants are endangered. If they die out, humans and animals will lose important sources of food, clean air, and a balanced environment. You can help protect plants like the Cumberland rosemary by teaching others about the importance of plants. Also, you can study about the endangered plants near you and work with others to protect them (National Geographic, 33). Plants are important and worth saving.

Sources:
<u>Cumberland Rosemary</u>. Fish and Wildlife Service.
<u>http://www.fws.gov/endangered/i/q/saq80.html</u> "Extinct and Endangered Species."
<u>Encyclopedia Americana</u>. Danbury: Grolier International, 1999.
Galan, Mark. <u>There's Still Time.</u> Washington, D.C.: National Geographic Society, 1997.

Learn new words. Write them in your personal dictionary.

B **Writing paragraphs. Write the correct paragraph from Abdul's report by each picture.**

Abdul's Research Report on Endangered Plants

DO NOT WRITE IN THIS BOOK

STEP–BY–STEP WRITING

Purpose: Explain a Topic

WRITING PROMPT

Research an endangered plant or animal that interests you. Write a research report explaining what the plant or animal is like, why it is endangered, and how people are helping it or can help it. Research in at least two different sources.

✔ **Prompt Checklist**

☐ I read the prompt carefully.
☐ I understood what the prompt asks me to do.

STEP 1 Pre-write

Look at Abdul's research notes. Take notes as you research. Follow Abdul's model.

Question: How many and which plants are endangered?

Paraphase:

Summarize: FWS lists nearly 750 plants. For example: Cumberland rosemary

Quote:

Source: *Endangered Species Program*, U.S. Fish and Wildlife Service, January 4, 2007 http://www.fws.gov/Endangered/

Page: http://ecos.fws.gov/tesspublic/SpeciesReport.do?dsource=plants

---

Question: Why are plants like the Cumberland rosemary important?

Paraphase:

Summarize:

Quote: "Furthermore, reduced plant growth and increased air pollution seem to be causing a build up of carbon dioxide (CO2) in the atmosphere."

Source: "Extinct and Endangered Species." *Encyclopedia Americana.* Danbury: Grolier International, 1999.

Page: 803

Question: What can people do to save plants like the Cumberland rosemary?

(Paraphase:) People can pass laws, teach others, and join with scientists to protect endangered plants.

Summarize:

Quote:

Source: Galan, Mark. *There's Still Time*. Washington, D.C.: National Geographic Society, 1997.

Page: 33

STEP 2 Organize

Look at Abdul's outline. Copy the outline or make one on a computer. Complete the outline with information from your research report.

Abdul's Outline

Title: Why the Cumberland rosemary Is Important

I. Introduction: Plants are endangered.
  A. How many? 750 species
  B. Cumberland rosemary is endangered and important.

II. Body: Endangered plants like the Cumberland rosemary are important.
  A. They give us/animals food.
  B. They give us clean air.
    1. Plants use carbon dioxide and give us oxygen.
  C. They are part of our environment.
    1. They help prevent floods.

III. Conclusion: What can we do?
  A. Teach others about endangered plants.
  B. Work with a group to help save plants near us.

STEP 3 Draft and Revise

A **Practice. Look at Abdul's first draft. How can he improve it? Answer the questions.**

Abdul's First Draft
Why the Cumberland Rosemary Is Important
(1) You have heard of endangered animals. (2) Did you know that plants are endangered too? (3) According to the U.S. Fish and Wildlife Service (FWS) Web site, there are nearly 750 endangered plants in North America. (4) There are three main reasons that animals and people need endangered plants like the Cumberland rosemary.
(5) Some of the endangered plants of North America are important to animals and people as food or medicine. (6) For instance, according to FWS, some birds and insects depend on Cumberland rosemary for food and habitat. (7) People also use rosemary as a spice.
(8) Another reason it is important is that it helps clean the air. (9) Like most plants, Cumberland rosemary takes in carbon dioxide in the air. (10) Then it gives off oxygen that people and animals breathe. (11) "Furthermore, reduced plant growth and increased air pollution seem to be causing a buildup of carbon dioxide (CO_2) in the atmosphere" (Encyclopedia Americana, 803). (12) The third reason Cumberland rosemary is important is that it is part of our ecosystem. (13) Cumberland rosemary grows on the banks of rivers in Tennessee and Kentucky. (14) There it helps stop floods. (15) If there is a flood, Cumberland rosemary's roots will help stop the dirt from moving. (16) Floods hurt animals, people, and property.
(17) Too many plants are endangered. (18) Humans and animals will lose important sources of food, clean air, and a balanced environment. (19) You can help protect plants like the Cumberland rosemary by teaching others about the importance of plants. (20) Also, you can study about the endangered plants near you and work with others to protect them. (21) Plants are important and worth saving.

1. How can Abdul best paraphrase the quote in sentence 11?

   A If plants like the Cumberland rosemary die out, then harmful gasses will build up in the air.

   B Carbon dioxide is also known as CO2.

   C Atmosphere means the gasses around the Earth.

   D Furthermore, reduced plant growth and increased air pollution seem to be causing a buildup of carbon dioxide (CO2) in the atmosphere.

2. What example phrase should Abdul add to the beginning of sentence 13?

   A For example,

   B Such as,

   C Like,

   D Including,

3. How can Abdul best rewrite sentence 16 to include more detail?

   A If floods hurt people, animals, and property.

   B Floods that are dangerous, hurt people, animals, and property.

   C Floods who are dangerous, hurt people, animals, and property.

   D Including, floods hurt people, animals, and property.

4. How can Abdul rewrite sentence 18 to show the condition and result of endangered plants?

   A If humans and animals lose important sources of food.

   B They will die out.

   C If they die out, humans and animals will lose important sources of food, clean air, and a balanced environment.

   D For instance, humans and animals will lose important sources of food, clean air, and a balanced environment.

B **Draft. Write a first draft for your research report. Use your notes from Steps 1 and 2.**

C **Revise. Read your first draft. How can you improve it? Look at the revision checklist. Revise your writing.**

✔ **Revision Checklist**

❑ I wrote introduction, body, and conclusion paragraphs.

❑ I wrote a thesis statement that summarized my three main points.

❑ I supported my points with evidence.

❑ I paraphrased or quoted my sources correctly.

❑ I used *if* clauses correctly.

❑ I used relative clauses with *who* and *that* correctly.

STEP 4 Edit

A **Practice. Look at the sentences. Choose the best word or phrase to complete each sentence.**

1. Giant pandas are _____endangered_____ animals from China.

   A endangered
   B species
   C sport
   D concerned

2. _____ the Chinese government doesn't protect them, they will become extinct.

   A Who
   B That
   C If
   D For example

3. Giant pandas _____ are born in zoos are healthy.

   A including
   B that
   C if
   D who

4. Your _____ can make a difference for these animals.

   A deer
   B efforts
   C survive
   D protect

B **Edit. Reread your draft from Step 3. Look at the editing checklist. Edit your writing.**

C **Peer Edit. Exchange drafts with a partner. Tell your partner what you like about the draft. Look at the editing checklist. Tell your partner how to improve the draft.**

STEP 5 Publish

Rewrite your report. Write in your best handwriting or use a computer. Look at Abdul's report on page 110 for ideas. Present your report to the class.

✔ Editing Checklist

me	my partner	
❑	❑	wrote introduction, body, and conclusion paragraphs
❑	❑	wrote a thesis statement that summarized my three main points
❑	❑	supported my points with evidence
❑	❑	paraphrased or quoted my sources correctly
❑	❑	used *if* clauses correctly
❑	❑	used relative clauses with *who* and *that* correctly

TECHNOLOGY

Researching Sources Online

Go to an online search engine. Do a keyword search for endangered plants. Narrow down your search using quotes around the topic or selecting only .edu or .gov sites. How many Web sites do you find? Which ones would be helpful for a report? Why? Read about endangered plants from two of the best Web sites. Compare the information from the two Web sites. Choose the best Web site on the topic. Then, tell the class about the Web site, what made it good, and the information you found there.

GROUP WRITING

Work in pairs to write about one of these topics. Follow the steps below.

1. Choose a topic.
2. Decide the form.
3. Do research if you need to.
4. Write a first draft.
5. Revise and edit the writing with your group.
6. Present your writing to the class.

Topic 1

Write about your English class. Compare and contrast this year's class with last year's. How are they different? How are they the same? How have you changed? Write three paragraphs.

Topic 2

Write about something in the rain forest. Choose an animal, plant, person, or event. Research your topic in at least two sources. Write three paragraphs about your rain forest topic.

TIMED WRITING

Choose one writing prompt. Complete the writing task in 45 minutes.

WRITING PROMPT 1

Write about an important activity in your life. How has this activity changed you? What were you like before you began the activity? What are you like now? Write three paragraphs to compare and contrast yourself before and after the activity.

WRITING PROMPT 2

Write about something related to the solar system. Choose a planet, scientist, or event. Research your topic in at least two sources. Write three paragraphs about your solar system topic.

 Test Tip

Remember structure! Remember that three-paragraph essays have thesis statements that tell the three main points of your essay. Then each point has examples or evidence to support it.

SELF-CHECK

Think about your writing skills. Check (✔) the answers that are true.

1. I understand . . .
   - ❏ words to describe change and experience.
   - ❏ words about the environment.

2. I can correctly use . . .
   - ❏ the simple past tense.
   - ❏ the past continuous tense.
   - ❏ past tense with *used to.*
   - ❏ *if* clauses.
   - ❏ relative clauses with *who* or *that.*

3. I can correctly . . .
   - ❏ make subjects and nouns agree.
   - ❏ paraphrase and quote from sources.

4. I can correctly . . .
   - ❏ use compare-and-contrast signal words.
   - ❏ support facts with evidence.

5. I can organize my writing in . . .
   - ❏ a three-paragraph essay with a thesis statement.
   - ❏ a three-paragraph research report.

6. I can write to . . .
   - ❏ compare and contrast.
   - ❏ explain a topic.

Unit 9

Write a Biography

UNIT OBJECTIVES

Writing
biographical narrative

Organization
timelines

Writing Strategies
outlining

Writing Conventions
citing sources

Vocabulary
conflict words

Grammar
parallel structure
passive voice

Technology
researching online celebrity
  biographies

Javier's Biography of Roberto Clemente

A **Discuss. Work with a partner. Talk about someone you admire and why you admire them.**

1. How do you know him/her?

2. Why do you admire him/her?

B **Read. Read Jennifer's biography of Anne Frank.**

Anne Frank

The person I admire most is Anne Frank. I read her diary this year in school. It was very sad. I have learned a lot from Anne Frank. She is my inspiration for being honest, loving my family, and living life fully.

Anne Frank was born in Germany in 1929 to Otto and Edith Frank. By 1933, her parents realized that Germany wasn't safe for Jews. The Frank family moved to the Netherlands when Anne was four years old. She lived there happily until she was eleven. In 1940, Hitler and the Nazis invaded the Netherlands. In 1942, like all other Jews, the Franks were asked to go to a "work camp." These were places with little food or protection, and lots of hard work. The Franks decided they would hide. On July 6, 1942, Anne Frank and her family moved into an attic over the Frank's old office. They lived there for more than two years. Anne was 13 to 15 years old. She wrote in her diary every day while she lived in hiding. At first she thought of the hiding as "an exciting adventure" (Jewish Virtual Library). But soon she became tired of living in darkness, silence, and secrecy. However, she cooperated and was helpful to her family even during the difficult times. She wrote about her feelings honestly in her diary. She wrote about her love for her family. She wrote about loving life and believing in the goodness of people (The Columbia Encyclopedia). On August 4, 1944, Nazi soldiers captured the Frank family. The family members were sent to separate concentration camps. Anne and her sister Margot were sent to Auschwitz for a month. Then, they were sent to another camp called Bergen-Belsen. In March, Anne and Margot died at Bergen-Belsen, just a few weeks before the Nazis were defeated.

Anne Frank's life was short and very difficult. When I read her diary, I understood her. Her thoughts and feelings sounded like mine. I write in my diary. I try to share my thoughts and feelings honestly. I love my family and try to help them. However, before I read Anne Frank's diary, I didn't understand about living life fully. Then, I read about her belief in people's goodness and the horrible way she died. I now know people can be good and people can be horrible. I now know that I should live every day as best as I can, like Anne Frank did.

Sources:

Anne Frank. The Columbia Encyclopedia. January 21, 2007.
    <http://www.bartleby.com/65/fr/Frank-An.html>

Anne Frank. The Jewish Virtual Library. January 21, 2007.
    <http://www.jewishvirtuallibrary.org/jsource/biography/frank.html>

Frank, Anne. The Diary of a Young Girl. New York: Bantam Books, 1993.

C **Write captions. Write a sentence for each picture on page 121. Use sentences from the reading.**

1. The person I admire most is Anne Frank.

2. _____

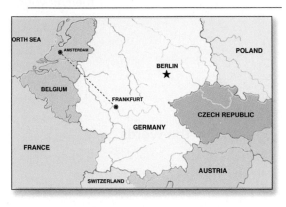

3. _____

4. _____

5. _____

6. _____

7. _____

8. _____

VOCABULARY

A Find each word in the reading on page 120. Look at the words around it to guess its meaning. Compare your answers with a partner.

Nouns	Verbs	Adjectives
adventure	admire	honest
concentration camp	capture	horrible
inspiration	die	impossible
protection	escape	sad
secrecy	hide	
soldiers	invade	
work camp		

Learn new words. Write them in your personal dictionary.

B Match the word with its definition. Write the definitions next to the words.

1. adventure _____
2. admire _____
3. honest _____
4. escape _____
5. impossible _____
6. secrecy _____
7. invade _____
8. horrible _____

a. to break free from capture
b. to look up to or be inspired
c. to enter by force
d. an exciting experience
e. completely truthful
f. completely terrible
g. not able to be done
h. keeping information private or hidden from others

C Write sentences with two or more vocabulary words.

1. Although work camps were horrible, concentration camps were even worse.
2. _____
3. _____
4. _____
5. _____

Parallel Structure

Verb Phrase Agreement	Noun Phrase Agreement
She is my inspiration for **being** honest, **loving** my family, and **living** life fully.	These were places with **little food, protection,** or **clothing**.

The verbs in a **verb phrase** must all agree or be the same form.
The nouns in a **noun phrase** must all agree or be the same form.

A Read the following sentences. Circle the phrases and label them as a noun or verb phrase.

1. But soon she became tired of living in darkness, silence, and secrecy. noun phrase

2. However, she cooperated and was helpful to her family. _____

3. Nazi soldiers came into the Frank's hiding place and captured the Frank family. _____

4. I love and try to help my family. _____

5. I try to share my thoughts and feelings honestly. _____

Active vs. Passive Voice

Active Voice	Passive Voice
The soldiers sent the family members to separate concentration camps.	**Anne and her sister Margot were sent** to a concentration camp called Auschwitz for a month (by the German soldiers).

Use the **active voice** to focus on the person who does the action.
Use the **passive voice** to focus on the receiver or the result of the action.

B Read the sentences below. Label each sentence *passive* or *active voice*. Rewrite the passive sentences to make them active.

1. Martin Luther King, Jr. was arrested. _____passive_____

   The police arrested Martin Luther King. _____

2. Martin Luther King, Jr. lead people even from jail. _____

   _____

3. He was followed and admired wherever he went. _____

   _____

ORGANIZATION

Timelines

Biographies are usually organized in chronological order. This means that the sequence of events is ordered by time. Timelines are horizontal lists of these important events.

Reread Jennifer's biography of Anne Frank on page 120. Complete Jennifer's timeline with the missing events in chronological order. Include dates when possible.

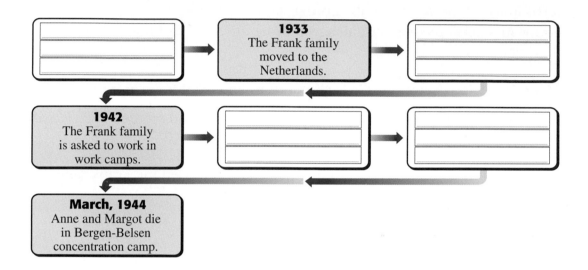

WRITING STRATEGIES

Outlining

Look at Jennifer's outline. Fill in the missing information.

Remember!
Graphic organizers like outlines help you plan and organize your ideas. In outlines, main ideas are numbered, supporting evidence and ideas are lettered.

Jennifer's Outline

Title: *Anne Frank*

I. Introduction: *The person I admire most is Anne Frank.*
  A. *We are different, but I read her diary and found it sad.*
  B. *I have learned a lot from Anne Frank.*
  C. *Thesis statement:* She is my inspiration for being honest, loving my family, and living life fully.

II. Body: *Anne Frank's life*
  A. *Birth date / parents*
  B. *Move to Netherlands*
  C.
  D. *Franks go into hiding*
  E. *Anne writes in her diary*
  F.
  G. *Franks are sent to concentration camps.*
  H.

III. Conclusion: *Why I admire Anne Frank*
  A. *Summarize/tell the meaning of her life*
  B. *Relate her life to mine*
  C.

WRITING CONVENTIONS

Citing Sources

Type of Reference	Citation
Books	Author. _Title of Book._ City of Publication: Publisher, Year.
	Frank, Anne. _The Diary of a Young Girl._ New York: Bantam Books, 1993.
Encyclopedias	Author of Article. (if given) "Article Title." _Title of Book._ City of Publication: Publisher, Year.
	"Anne Frank." _The Columbia Encyclopedia._ Washington, D.C.: 2006.
Web sites	Creator's Name. (if given) _Web Page Title._ Institution or organization. Date of access <URL network address>.
	If you cannot find the information, use the Web address as the citation.
	Anne Frank. The Jewish Virtual Library. January 21, 2007. <http://www.jewishvirtuallibrary.org/jsource/biography/frank.html>

Look at Jennifer's sources to answer the following questions.

1. What is the name of Anne Frank's diary?

_____

2. Who published Anne Frank's diary?

_____

3. How many Web sites did Jennifer use to research her biography?

_____

4. What is the article title in The Columbia Encyclopedia?

_____

Write a Biography

> **Biographies** are true stories about someone's life, written by another person. Biographies list important dates, events, and people in the person's life.

  A **Read.** Javier's biography of Roberto Clemente.

Learn new words. Write them in your personal dictionary.

Roberto Clemente

Roberto Clemente is my hero. Roberto and I have a lot in common. Roberto loved baseball, which is my favorite sport. Roberto is Puerto Rican, like me. Roberto loved his two home countries as I do. Roberto Clemente was a great baseball player, a good husband and father, and a generous man.

Roberto Clemente was born on August 18, 1934 in Puerto Rico. As a child, he was excellent at many sports, but his favorite was baseball. He first played in Puerto Rico. Then, he played for the Brooklyn Dodgers, but only in their minor league. In 1955 he joined the Pittsburgh Pirates major league. He was an excellent professional baseball player. He played in two World Series. He won the National League Batting Championship four times for great batting. He won twelve Golden Gloves for excellent outfield catching. But Roberto Clemente wasn't just a great baseball player. He was a good husband and father. In 1964, he married Vera Cristina Zabala. Together they had three sons, all born in Puerto Rico. Roberto Clemente loved his family and loved his two countries, but he also loved strangers. Roberto Clemente was a generous man. In 1972 there was a horrible earthquake in Nicaragua. Roberto Clemente got on a plane to bring medicine, food, and clothing to Nicaragua. The weather was bad. But Roberto Clemente wanted to make sure the supplies got to Nicaragua. On December 31, 1972, the plane crashed on the way to Nicaragua. Roberto Clemente's body was never found.

Roberto Clemente is my hero because I want to be like him when I grow up. I hope to play baseball well. I hope to be a good husband and a good father. I hope to show my love and respect for my family and my two home countries. Most of all, I hope to show my generosity for strangers. I want to grow up to be like my hero Roberto Clemente.

Sources:
Powell, Kimberly and Albrecht. <u>Roberto Clemente.</u> About: Pittsburgh, PA, 2007.
   http://pittsburgh.about.com/od/pirates/p/clemente.htm
<u>Roberto Clemente.</u> National Baseball Hall of Fame, 2007.
   http://www.baseballhalloffame.org/hofers_and_honorees/hofer_bios/Clemente_Roberto.htm

B **Writing paragraphs.** Write the correct paragraph from Javier's biography by each picture.

Javier's Biography of Roberto Clemente

DO NOT WRITE IN THIS BOOK

STEP–BY–STEP WRITING

Purpose: Describe Someone's Life

WRITING PROMPT

Write a three-paragraph biography about a person you admire. Research their lives in at least two sources. If you are writing about someone you know well, sources may be people who also know that person or the person him/herself.

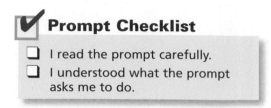

Prompt Checklist

❑ I read the prompt carefully.
❑ I understood what the prompt asks me to do.

STEP 1 Pre-write

Look at Javier's timeline. Make notes on a timeline as you research. Follow Javier's model.

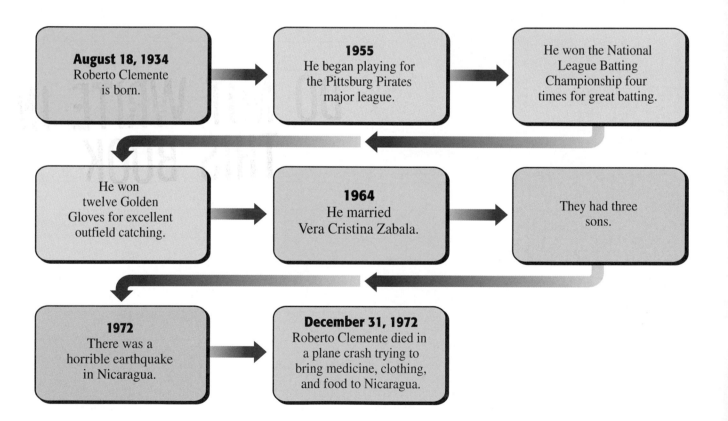

August 18, 1934
Roberto Clemente is born.

1955
He began playing for the Pittsburg Pirates major league.

He won the National League Batting Championship four times for great batting.

He won twelve Golden Gloves for excellent outfield catching.

1964
He married Vera Cristina Zabala.

They had three sons.

1972
There was a horrible earthquake in Nicaragua.

December 31, 1972
Roberto Clemente died in a plane crash trying to bring medicine, clothing, and food to Nicaragua.

STEP 2 Organize

Look at Javier's outline. Copy the outline or make one on a computer. Complete the outline with information from your biography.

Javier's Outline

Title: Roberto Clemente

I. Introduction: Roberto Clemente is my hero.
   A. We both love Puerto Rico and the U.S.
   B. We both play baseball
   C. Roberto was excellent at baseball, a great husband, and a generous man.

II. Body: Roberto Clemente's life
   A. Excellent at baseball: played for the Pittsburg Pirates, won 4 Batting Champs, won 12 golden gloves
   B. Loving husband and father
   C. Generous to people in need – died trying to go to Nicaragua to bring supplies to earthquake victims

III. Conclusion: I hope to be like him
   A. I hope to be a good baseball player
   B. I hope to be a good father and husband
   C. I hope to be kind to others

A **Practice. Look at Javier's first draft. How can he improve it? Answer the questions.**

JAVIER'S FIRST DRAFT

Roberto Clemente

(1) Roberto Clemente is my hero. (2) Roberto and I have a lot in common. (3) Roberto loved baseball, which is my favorite sport. (4) Roberto is Puerto Rican, like me. (5) Roberto loved his two home countries as I do.

(6) Roberto Clemente was born on August 18, 1934 in Puerto Rico. (7) As a child, he was excellent at many sports, but his favorite was baseball. (8) He first played in Puerto Rico. (9) Then he played for the Brooklyn Dodgers, but only in their minor league. (10) In 1955 he joined the Pittsburgh Pirates major league. (11) He was an excellent professional baseball player. (12) Roberto played on sand fields in Puerto Rico until he was 18 years old. (13) He played in two World Series. (14) He won the National League Batting Championship four times for great batting. (15) He won twelve Golden Gloves for excellent outfield catching. (16) But Roberto Clemente wasn't just a great baseball player. (17) He was a good husband and father. (18) In 1964, he married Vera Cristina Zabala. (19) Together they had three sons, all born in Puerto Rico. (20) Roberto Clemente loved his family and loved his two countries, but he also loved strangers. (21) Roberto Clemente was a generous man. (22) In 1972, there was a horrible earthquake in Nicaragua. (23) Roberto Clemente got on a plane to bring medicine, food, and clothing to Nicaragua. (24) The weather was bad. (25) But Roberto Clemente wanted to make sure the supplies got to Nicaragua. (26) On December 31, 1972, the plane crashed on the way to Nicaragua. (27) Nobody ever found Roberto Clemente's body.

(28) Roberto Clemente is my hero because I want to be like him when I grow up. (29) I hope to play baseball well. (30) I hope to be a good husband and a good father. (31) I hope to show my love and respect for my family and my two home countries, Puerto Rico and the United States. (32) Most of all, I hope to show my generosity for strangers. (33) I want to grow up to be like my hero Roberto Clemente.

Sources:

(33) "Powell, Kimberly and Albrecht." <u>Roberto Clemente.</u> About: Pittsburgh, PA, 2007. http://
pittsburgh.about.com/od/pirates/p/clemente.htm

(34) <u>Roberto Clemente.</u> National Baseball Hall of Fame, 2007.
http://www.baseballhalloffame.org/
hofers_and_honorees/hofer_bios/Clemente_Roberto.htm

1. Which is the best thesis statement for Javier's biography?
   A Roberto Clemente is my hero.
   B I want to grow up to be like my hero Roberto Clemente.
   C Roberto Clemente was a great baseball player, a good husband and father, and a generous man.
   D Roberto Clemente was a great baseball player.

2. Which sentence in paragraph 2 is out of chronological order?
   A Sentence 10
   B Sentence 12
   C Sentence 14
   D Sentence 16

3. How can Javier rewrite sentence 27 so that it is in the passive voice?
   A Roberto Clemente's body was never found.
   B People never found Roberto Clemente's body.
   C His family never found Roberto Clemente's body.
   D Someone did find Roberto Clemente's body.

4. How can Javier correctly rewrite source 35?
   A Powell, Kimberly and Albrecht. "Roberto Clemente." About: Pittsburgh, PA, 2007. http://pittsburgh.about.com/od/pirates/p/clemente.htm
   B Powell, Kimberly and Albrecht. "Roberto Clemente. About: Pittsburgh, PA, 2007. http://pittsburgh.about.com/od/pirates/p/clemente.htm"
   C Powell, Kimberly and Albrecht. Roberto Clemente. About: Pittsburgh, PA, 2007. http://pittsburgh.about.com/od/pirates/p/clemente.htm
   D Powell, Kimberly and Albrecht. Roberto Clemente. About: Pittsburgh, PA, 2007. http://pittsburgh.about.com/od/pirates/p/clemente.htm

B Draft. Write a first draft for your biography. Use your notes from Steps 1 and 2.

C Revise. Read your first draft. How can you improve it? Look at the revision checklist. Revise your writing.

Revision Checklist

❏ I wrote introduction, body, and conclusion paragraphs.
❏ I wrote a thesis statement that summarized my three main points.
❏ I wrote the events in chronological order.
❏ I paraphrased or quoted my sources correctly.
❏ I used parallel structure for noun and verb phrases.
❏ I used passive voice correctly.

STEP 4 Edit

A Practice. Look at the sentences. Choose the best substitute for the underlined words. If the sentence is correct, choose "Make no change."

1. Jackie Chan is my hero because he is strong, determined, and <u>he has a lot of success as a movie star</u>.

   A he had a lot of success as a movie star

   B he is going to have a lot of success as a movie star

   Ⓒ a successful movie star

   D Make no change.

2. Jackie Chan is <u>a protection</u> for me because he is an excellent martial artist and a talented movie maker.

   A an admirer

   B a secrecy

   C an inspiration

   D Make no change.

3. At birth, Jackie Chan <u>had named Chan Kong-Sang by his parents</u>.

   A Jackie Chan's parents named him Chan Kong-Sang

   B Jackie Chan is named Chan Kong-Sang

   C Jackie Chan has named Chan Kong-Sang by his parents

   D Make no change.

4. Jackie Chan speaks seven languages, creates movies, and <u>performs all</u> his own stunts.

   A the performer of all

   B performed all

   C performing all

   D Make no change.

B Edit. Reread your draft from Step 3. Look at the editing checklist. Edit your writing.

C Peer Edit. Exchange drafts with a partner. Tell your partner what you like about the draft. Look at the editing checklist. Tell your partner how to improve the draft.

STEP 5 Publish

Rewrite your biography in your best handwriting or on a computer. Look at Javier's biography on page 126 for ideas. Present your biography to the class.

✔ Editing Checklist

my		
me	partner	
☐	☐	wrote introduction, body, and conclusion paragraphs
☐	☐	supported my points with evidence from the person's life
☐	☐	cited my sources correctly
☐	☐	used noun and verb phrases that agree
☐	☐	used passive and active voice correctly

TECHNOLOGY

Researching Online Celebrity Biographies

Go to an online search engine. Do a **keyword search** for your favorite celebrity. Before clicking on the Web sites you found, evaluate the source. Is it reliable? Most reliable sources are encyclopedias or most museum pages. Find at least two reliable sources. Take notes on a timeline. Then, write a one-paragraph biography of your favorite celebrity.

Unit 10

Response to Literature

Writing
write a review of literature

Organization
analyzing strengths and weaknesses

Writing Strategies
expressing opinion

Writing Conventions
adjective formation

Vocabulary
literary analysis words

Grammar
compound subjects/predicates
adjective phrases

Technology
researching online book reviews

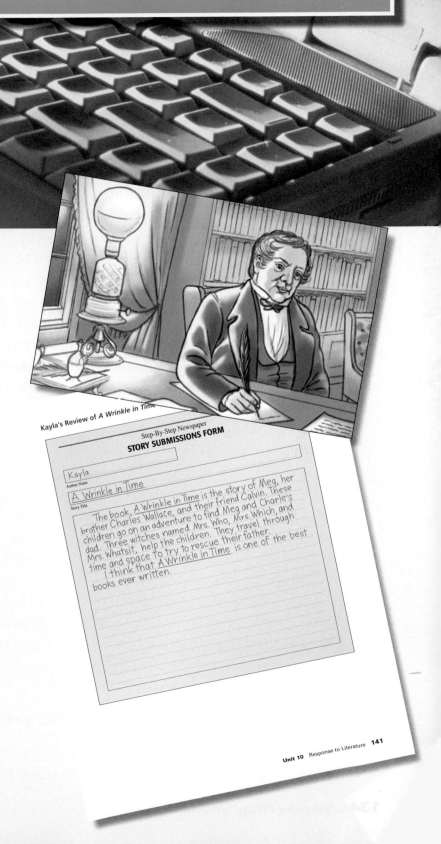

Kayla's Review of A Wrinkle in Time

Step-By-Step Newspaper
STORY SUBMISSIONS FORM

Kayla
Author Name

A Wrinkle in Time
Story Title

The book, A Wrinkle in Time is the story of Meg, her brother Charles Wallace, and their friend Calvin. These children go on an adventure to find Meg and Charlie's dad. Three witches named Mrs. Who, Mrs. Which, and Mrs. Whatsit, help the children. They travel through time and space to try to rescue their father.
I think that A Wrinkle in Time is one of the best books ever written.

READING

A **Discuss. Work with a partner. Talk about a book you have read and enjoyed recently.**

1. What is the name of the book?

2. Why did you like the book?

B **Read. Read Jennifer's literature review.**

The Legend of Sleepy Hollow—A Great Story, Not a Great Scare!

Washington Irving wrote a great story called, "The Legend of Sleepy Hollow." I think that it is very well written, but it probably won't scare you as it did its main character, Ichabod Crane. "The Legend of Sleepy Hollow" is the story of the little town of Sleepy Hollow. It was a farming town on the Hudson River. Farmers didn't have much money to send their children to school. So, they only paid the schoolteacher, Ichabod Crane, a little bit, and then let him stay in their homes and eat their food. He lived one week in each farmer's home. Ichabod was a good teacher and a helpful man. He helped the farmers in the fields and helped the wives take care of the children. When the work was done, he loved to sit by the fire and listen to ghost stories. The scariest story was about a headless ghost who rode a horse through town. After story time, Ichabod walked home. He often heard a loud rush of wind and thought that the headless horseman was after him! That is how Washington Irving ends his story.

I consider that "The Legend of Sleepy Hollow" is an excellent story with few weaknesses. It seems to me that the story's greatest strength is Irving's descriptive writing. For example, Irving describes Ichabod Crane as a crane. First, Irving uses exaggeration, writing that Ichabod's hands "dangled a mile out of his sleeves." This exaggeration helps the reader see that his arms were very long. Next, Irving uses funny words to make his images clear. For instance, he compares Ichabod's feet to shovels. I believe that another strength of the story is that it is realistic. The characters, setting, and plot are believable. For example, the farmers work hard on the farm. The wives spin yarn and tell stories. Ichabod is helpful, hungry, and interested in ghost stories. This funny combination makes him seem like a real person. All of this information makes the story realistic. The only parts of the story that aren't realistic are the ghost stories. I feel that this is the greatest weakness of the story. The ghost story of the headless horseman is supposed to be scary. Yet, the reader is not scared by the ghost story. Washington Irving writes a very good, but not a very scary story.

Even though his story may not scare you, I believe that it will thrill you. Washington Irving's clear descriptions and realistic characters, plots, and settings make "The Legend of Sleepy Hollow" an excellent story. I would recommend it to anyone who wants a good story, but not a good scare!

C **Write captions. Write a sentence for each picture on page 135. Use sentences from the reading.**

1. Washington Irving wrote a great story called, "The Legend of Sleepy Hollow."

2. _____

3. _____

4. _____

5. _____

6. _____

7. _____

8. _____

VOCABULARY

A Find each word in the reading on page 134. Look at the words around it to guess its meaning. Compare your answers with a partner.

Nouns		Verbs		Adjectives
characters	plot	believe	feel	realistic
descriptions	setting	consider	recommend	clear
exaggeration	strength	compare	seem	excellent
images	weakness	describe	thrill	

Learn new words. Write them in your personal dictionary.

B Use the clues to complete the crossword puzzle.

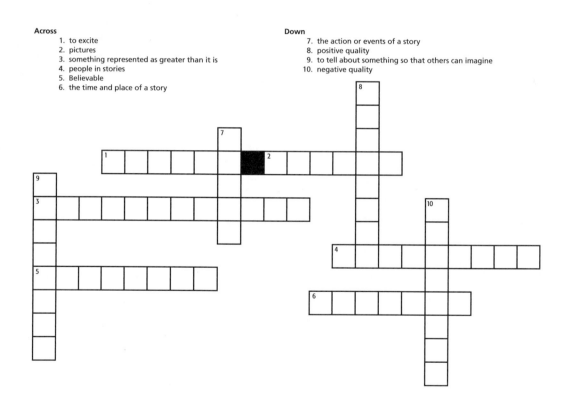

Across
1. to excite
2. pictures
3. something represented as greater than it is
4. people in stories
5. Believable
6. the time and place of a story

Down
7. the action or events of a story
8. positive quality
9. to tell about something so that others can imagine
10. negative quality

C Complete the sentences below with words from the vocabulary list above.

1. The story "The Legend of Sleepy Hollow" gave me quite a _____thrill_____.

2. The _____ isn't that exciting. Nothing much happens in the story.

3. Yet the _____ in the story are such believable people.

4. But Washington Irving's greatest _____ is his ability to create _____ in the reader's mind.

5. The story's only _____ is that it isn't very scary.

Step–by–Step Writing Book 2

Compound Subjects and Predicates		
Sentences with Simple Subjects and Predicates	**Sentences with Compound Subjects**	**Sentences with Compound Predicates**
Ichabod was a good teacher and a helpful man.	**The farmers, the wives, and the children** liked Ichabod.	He **helped** the farmers in the fields and **helped** the wives take care of the children.
I believe that another strength of the story is that it is realistic.	**The characters, setting, and plot** are believable.	The wives **spin** yarn and **tell** stories.

Compound means more than one. **Compound subjects** mean more than one noun performs the action in a sentence.

A compound predicate consists of more than one verb or verb phrase being performed in the sentence.

A Read the following sentences. Circle the subject and underline the predicate. Write *compound subject* and/or *compound predicate* on the line.

1. (Ichabod) stayed in their homes and ate their food. ___compound predicate___

2. He sat by the fire and listened to ghost stories. _____

3. Exaggeration and funny words make Irving's descriptions clear. _____

4. The story didn't scare me or bore me. _____

5. Washington Irving's clear descriptions and realistic characters, plots, and settings make "The Legend of Sleepy Hollow" an excellent story. _____

B Complete the following sentences with a compound subject or a compound predicate. Use your imagination and information from the story.

1. ____Jennifer and her friend Keesha____ read the story of "The Legend of Sleepy Hollow."

2. During the day, Ichabod _____.

3. At night, _____ told stories around the fire.

4. After telling stories, Ichabod _____.

5. _____ make Irving a great writer.

Adjective Phrases

Sentence	Noun	Adjective Phrase
Sleepy Hollow was a farming town.	Sleepy Hollow	a farming town
He often heard a loud rush of wind.	wind	a loud rush of

Adjective phrases are phrases that describe nouns. The adjective phrase can describe the subject or another noun in the sentence. Adjective phrases help you tell more about a noun.

C Circle the adjective(s) that describe(s) the underlined noun. Write adjective(s) or adjective phrase(s) after each sentence.

1. <u>Ichabod Crane</u> was (a good teacher and a helpful man.) _____adjective phrase_____

2. "<u>The Legend of Sleepy Hollow</u>" is an excellent story with few weaknesses.
   _____

3. The <u>images</u> are vivid and clear. _____

4. Irving describes <u>Ichabod Crane</u> as a crane._____

5. The <u>characters</u> seem familiar and believable. _____

ORGANIZATION

Analyzing Strengths and Weaknesses

Strengths are positive qualities. **Weaknesses** are negative qualities. All stories and books have strengths and weaknesses. To find the strengths and weaknesses of a story or book, think about why it is (or is not) a good piece of literature. Then, think about how the story or book may be improved.

A Complete Jennifer's strength and weakness chart based on the literature review on page 134.

Title: "The Legend of Sleepy Hollow"

Strengths	Weaknesses
descriptive writing	

WRITING STRATEGIES

Expressing Opinion

When you **express your opinion**, you say what you think or feel about a subject. Your opinions are not facts, but they may be supported by evidence from the book or story. The following phrases tell the reader that you are about to express an opinion:

In my opinion	*I think that*	*I believe*
I feel that	*I consider*	*It seems to me*

Skim Jennifer's literature review on page 134 for examples of each phrase for expressing opinion. Copy the sentence next to the phrase.

1. In my opinion: In my opinion, it is a perfect story to read on a late fall night.

2. I think that: _____

3. I consider: _____

4. It seems to me: _____

5. I feel that: _____

6. I believe: _____

WRITING CONVENTIONS

Adjective Formation

You can make adjectives from base words by adding one of the following endings: *-ing, -ed, -y.*

    farm → farm**ing**   interest → interest**ed**   scare → scar**y**

Change the base words into adjectives by adding one of the endings. Skim Jennifer's literature review if you need help.

Base words	Adjective Form(s)	Base words	Adjective Form(s)
exaggerate	exaggerating	interest	
scare		sleep	
hunger		fun	
help		farm	

Write a Review of Literature

For a three-paragraph literature review, the introduction paragraph tells the title, author, setting, characters, and basic plot of the story or book. The body paragraph tells the strengths and weaknesses, citing examples for each one. The conclusion paragraph gives a summary of your ideas and tells why the reader should or should not read the book or story.

  A **Read.** Read Kayla's review of the book *A Wrinkle in Time*.

A Wrinkle in Time

My favorite author, Madeline L'Engle, wrote a book called <u>A Wrinkle in Time</u>. It is the story of Meg, her brother Charles Wallace, and their friend Calvin. These children go on an adventure to find Meg and Charles' dad. Three witches named Mrs. Who, Mrs. Which, and Mrs. Whatsit, help the children. They travel through time and space to try to rescue their father. You will have to read the book to see if they succeed.

When you read it, I think that you will agree that <u>A Wrinkle in Time</u> is one of the best books ever written. In my opinion, its greatest strength is that it combines reality, fantasy, and science fiction all in one book. The reality is in the characters and their feelings. Meg, Charles Wallace, and Calvin are very normal children. Well, Charles Wallace is very smart. But all three argue like normal children. They are afraid like real kids. Although they act, talk, and seem like real children, they go on a very unreal adventure. This is the fantasy part of the story. I consider that Madeline L'Engle is one of the best fantasy writers ever. She tells such a wonderful story of adventure, witches, and good vs. evil. It seems to me that the science fiction part of the book is its strength and its weakness. In <u>A Wrinkle in Time</u>, Madeline L'Engle describes time travel very well, but sometimes it is hard to understand. I feel that this is the book's only weakness. But I know that won't stop you from enjoying this great book.

I believe if you like realism, fantasy, or science fiction you will love Madeline L'Engle's book <u>A Wrinkle in Time</u>. Even though it is confusing in some parts, the real characters and their fantastic adventures through time and space will make you want to read the book quickly. Then, you will have to find the next book in the series.

Learn new words. Write them in your personal dictionary.

B **Writing Paragraphs.** Kayla must shorten her review to publish it in the school newspaper. Help her write only the important information.

Kayla's Review of *A Wrinkle in Time*

STORY SUBMISSIONS FORM

Kayla

Author Name

A Wrinkle in Time

Story Title

    The book, A Wrinkle in Time is the story of Meg, her brother Charles Wallace, and their friend Calvin. These children go on an adventure to find Meg and Charle's dad. Three witches named Mrs. Who, Mrs. Which, and Mrs. Whatsit, help the children. They travel through time and space to try to rescue their father.
    I think that A Wrinkle in Time is one of the best books ever written.

STEP-BY-STEP WRITING

Purpose: Write a Review of Literature

WRITING PROMPT

Write a three-paragraph literature review about a book or story you read recently. In the introduction paragraph, write the title and author and briefly describe the characters, setting, and plot. In the body paragraph, express opinions about the strengths and weaknesses of the book or story. Support each opinion with at least one example from the book or story. In the conclusion paragraph, give a summary of your ideas and tell why the reader should or should not read the book or story.

✔ Prompt Checklist

☐ I read the prompt carefully.
☐ I understood what the prompt asks me to do.

STEP 1 Pre-write

Look at Kayla's strengths/weaknesses chart. Take notes as you read. Follow Kayla's model.

Title: _A Wrinkle in Time_

Strengths	Weaknesses
Realistic characters and feelings	Science fiction descriptions are sometimes
Excellent fantasy story	confusing and difficult to understand.
Good science fiction adventure	

Title:

Strengths	Weaknesses

STEP 2 Organize

Look at Kayla's outline. Copy the outline or make one on a computer. Complete the outline with information from your literature review.

Kayla's Outline

Title: A Wrinkle in Time

I. Introduction
  A. Title: A Wrinkle in Time
  B. Author: Madeline L'Engle
  C. Setting: through time and space
  D. Characters: Meg, Charles Wallace, Calvin, their father, Mrs. Whatsit, Mrs. Who, Mrs. Which
  E. Plot: with the help of the witches, the children find their father

II. Body
  A. Strengths: reality, fantasy, and science fiction all in one
  B. Weakness: science fiction is hard to understand

III. Conclusion
  A. Summarise my ideas
  B. Recommend the book: definitely

STEP 3 Draft and Revise

A **Practice. Look at Kayla's first draft. How can she improve it? Answer the questions.**

Kayla's First Draft

A Wrinkle in Time

(1) My favorite author, Madeline L'Engle, wrote a book called _A Wrinkle in Time_. (2) It is the story of Meg, her brother Charles Wallace, and their friend Calvin. (3) These children go on an adventure to find Meg and Charles' dad. (4) Three witches named Mrs. Who, Mrs. Which, and Mrs. Whatsit, help the children. (5) They travel through time and space to try to rescue their father. (6) You will have to read the book to see if they succeed. (7) In my opinion, its greatest strength is that it combines reality, fantasy, and science fiction all in one book.

(8) When you read it, I think that you will agree that _A Wrinkle in Time_ is one of the best books ever written. (9) The reality is in the people and their feelings. Meg, Charles Wallace, and Calvin are very normal children. (10) Although they seem like real children, they go on a very unreal adventure. (11) This is the fantasy part of the story. (12) I consider that Madeline L'Engle is one of the best fantasy writers ever. (13) She tells such a wonderful story of adventure, witches, and good vs. evil. (14) The science fiction part of the book is its strength and its weakness. (15) In _A Wrinkle in Time_, Madeline L'Engle describes time travel, a very popular topic of science fiction. (16) I think L'Engle describes the time travel very well, but sometimes it is hard to understand. (17) I feel that this is the book's only weakness. (18) But I know that won't stop you from enjoying this great book.

(19) I believe if you like realism, fantasy, or science fiction you will love Madeline L'Engle's book _A Wrinkle in Time_. (20) Even though it is confusing in some parts, the real characters and their fantastic adventures through time and space will make you want to read the book quickly. (21) Then, you will have to find the next book in the series. (22) I am so happy that Madeline L'Engle wrote three books about these great characters and their wild adventures.

---

1. Which sentence from paragraph 1 should be moved to paragraph 2?

   A Sentence 3
   B Sentence 4
   C Sentence 6
   D Sentence 7

2. What vocabulary word should Kayla use instead of *people* in sentence 9?

   A characters
   B images
   C plot
   D setting

3. What compound predicate should Kayla add before *seem* in sentence 10?

   A the children and the witches
   B are very realistic
   C act, talk, and
   D exaggerate, describe, and

4. What phrase can Kayla add to the beginning of sentence 14 to show that she is expressing her opinion?

   A The best writer in the world,
   B It seems to me that
   C It is a fact that
   D Everyone says that

B **Draft.** Write a first draft for your literature review. Use your notes from Steps 1 and 2.

C **Revise.** Read your first draft. How can you improve it? Look at the revision checklist. Revise your writing.

✔ Revision Checklist

- ❏ I wrote introduction, body, and conclusion paragraphs.
- ❏ I included the title and author in the first paragraph.
- ❏ I briefly described the plot, characters, and setting in the first paragraph.
- ❏ I wrote about the strengths and weaknesses of the book or story in the second paragraph.
- ❏ I supported these opinions with evidence from the book or story.
- ❏ I used expressing opinions phrases with each opinion.
- ❏ I summarized my ideas and recommended the book in the third paragraph.

STEP 4 Edit

A **Practice.** Look at the sentences. Choose the best word or phrase to complete each sentence.

1. The book <u>Sadako and the Thousand Paper Cranes</u> is very _____.

   (A) moving
   B movie
   C moved
   D mover

2. _____ that it is the best book I have ever read.

   A I consider
   B I think that
   C I believe that
   D I seem

3. Sadako is _____.

   A a kind, brave, and smart
   B kind, brave, and girl
   C kind and smart girl
   D a kind, brave, and smart girl

4. The _____ of the story is Japan in 1955.

   A characters
   B setting
   C plot
   D weakness

B **Edit.** Reread your draft from Step 3. Look at the editing checklist. Edit your writing.

C **Peer Edit.** Exchange drafts with a partner. Tell your partner what you like about the draft. Look at the editing checklist. Tell your partner how to improve the draft.

STEP 5 Publish

Rewrite your review. Write in your best handwriting or use a computer. Look at Kayla's review on page 140 for ideas. Present your review to the class.

✔ Editing Checklist

my		
me	partner	
❑	❑	used adjectives and adjective phrases correctly
❑	❑	used compound predicates and subjects correctly
❑	❑	used expressing opinion phrases correctly

TECHNOLOGY

Researching Online Book Reviews

Most online bookstores offer book reviews of their books. There are also online book review sites. Go to an online bookstore or book review site. Type in your favorite book. Read and analyze the reviews. Are they three-paragraph reviews? If not, what form are they in? Do they use expressing opinion phrases? If so, which ones? Do they support their opinions with evidence from the book? Do they recommend the book? Take notes. Repeat this process with at least two more sites. Share your notes with the class.

GROUP WRITING

Work in pairs to write about one of these topics. Follow the steps below.

1. Choose a topic.
2. Decide the form.
3. Do research if you need to.
4. Write a first draft.
5. Revise and edit the writing with your group.
6. Present your writing to the class.

Topic 1

Write about your favorite teacher. Why is he/she your favorite? What is he/she like? Write any biographical information about his/her life that shows why this teacher is important to you.

Topic 2

Write about your favorite story or book. Who wrote it? What are the characters, setting, and plot? What are its strengths and weaknesses? Would you recommend it? Why or why not?

DO NOT WRITE IN THIS BOOK

TIMED WRITING

Choose one writing prompt. Complete the writing task in 45 minutes.

WRITING PROMPT 1

Write about your favorite family member. Why is he/she your favorite? What is he/she like? Write any biographical information about his/her life that shows why this person is important to you.

WRITING PROMPT 2

Write about your favorite book. Who wrote it? What are the characters, setting, and plot? What are its strengths and weaknesses? Would you recommend it? Why or why not?

🕐 Test Tip

Remember Organization! Remember that three-paragraph essays can be planned and organized using an outline. In outlines, numbers introduce main ideas and letters give supporting evidence.

SELF-CHECK

Think about your writing skills. Check (✔) the answers that are true.

1. I understand . . .
   - ❏ words that describe conflict and difficult times.
   - ❏ words for literature reviews.

2. I can correctly use . . .
   - ❏ parallel structure.
   - ❏ passive voice.
   - ❏ compound subjects.
   - ❏ compound predicates.
   - ❏ adjective phrases.

3. I can correctly . . .
   - ❏ cite sources.
   - ❏ form adjectives.

4. I can correctly . . .
   - ❏ outline.
   - ❏ express opinions.

5. I can organize my writing . . .
   - ❏ in chronological order.
   - ❏ by its strengths and weaknesses.

6. I can write to . . .
   - ❏ describe someone's life.
   - ❏ review literature.

NOUNS

Nouns name a person, place, or thing.

Regular Plural Nouns

Nouns can be **singular** (*one*) or **plural** (*more than one*).

To make most nouns plural, add *s* or *es* after the singular noun.

Singular	Plural	Rule
bedroom book	bedroom**s** book**s**	most nouns: add **s**
class lunch	class**es** lunch**es**	nouns that end in **s, ch, sh, x,** or **z**: add **es**
famil**y** lad**y**	famil**ies** lad**ies**	nouns that end in a **consonant+y**: change the **y** to **i** and add **es**

Irregular Plural Nouns

Some nouns are **irregular** in the plural form.

Singular	Irregular Plural
man	men
woman	women
child	children
mouse	mice
foot	feet
tooth	teeth

Count and Noncount Nouns

Count nouns are nouns you can count. They are singular or plural.

Use **a, an, the,** or a number with count nouns.

Noncount nouns can't be counted. They are singular.

Don't use **a, an,** or numbers. Use **some** for a non-specific amount.

Count	Noncount
I have a banana.	I have lettuce.
I have eight oranges.	Buy some cheese.
Cut up the tomato.	Cut up some cheese.

Articles

Use an **article** before count nouns.

Article	Rule	Example
a, an	before general, singular count nouns use *a* before consonants use *an* before vowels	Francisco is **a** student. There is **a** book. I eat **an** apple every day.
the	before specific nouns when there is only one	I saw a movie. **The** movie was good. There is **the** Lincoln Memorial.

Possessive Nouns

Possessive nouns show ownership.

Sentence	Sentence with Possessive Noun	Rule
Francisco has a small bedroom.	**Francisco's** bedroom is small.	Add apostrophe + s ('s) to names.
The **boy** has a new poster.	The **boy's** poster is new.	Add apostrophe + s ('s) to singular nouns.
The **girls** have gym class now.	The **girls'** gym class is now.	Add apostrophe (') to regular plural nouns.
The **men** have blue hats.	The **men's** hats are blue.	Add apostrophe + s ('s) to irregular plural nouns.

PRONOUNS

A pronoun takes the place of a noun or refers to a noun.

Example: <u>My brother</u> is sick today. <u>He</u> has a cold.

Subject Pronouns (p. 49)

A subject pronoun takes the place of a subject noun. It does the action in a sentence.

Subject Pronoun	Sentence
I	**I** am sick today.
you	**You** are a student.
he/she	**She** plays soccer.
it	**It** is large.
we	**We** read the news.
you	**You** are students.
they	**They** are busy.

Contractions

I am = **I'm**

you are = **you're**

he is = **he's**

she is = **she's**

it is = **it's**

we are = **we're**

they are = **they're**

Object Pronouns (pp. 49, 64)

Object pronouns take the place of object nouns. They show to whom something happened or who got something. They come after a verb or preposition.

Object Pronoun	Sentence
me	Please help **me** understand.
you	Fatima works with **you**.
him/her	A woman is talking to **him**.
it	People are next to **it**.
us	They live next door to **us**.
you	The teacher will give information to **you**.
them	The mother is watching **them**.

VERBS

A **verb** is an action word.

Simple Present Tense (p. 5)

Use the **simple present tense** to tell about an action that is true now or that generally happens.

Simple Present Tense			
Affirmative		**Negative**	
I You We They	**work** on Saturdays.	I You We They	**do not work** on Saturdays.
He She It	**works** every day.	He She It	**does not work** every day.

Contractions

does not = **doesn't**

do not = **don't**

Rule

Add an **-s** to a verb for **he, she,** and **it.**

Present Continuous Tense (p. 33)

Use the **present continuous tense** to talk about an action happening right now.
Use **be** and a main verb. Add **-ing** to the end of the verb.

Present Continuous Tense	
Affirmative	**Negative**
I **am eating** right now.	I **am not eating** right now.
You **are reading** right now.	You **are not reading** right now.
He **is writing** right now.	He **is not writing** right now.
We **are dancing** right now.	We **are not dancing** right now.
They **are running** right now.	They **are not running** right now.

Contractions

I am = **I'm**

you are = **you're**

he is = **he's**

she is = **she's**

it is = **it's**

we are = **we're**

they are = **they're**

is not = **isn't**

are not = **aren't**

Simple Past Tense (pp. 5, 93)

Use the **simple past tense** of a verb to tell about an action that happened in the past.

Simple Past Tense	
Affirmative	**Negative**
Francisco **helped** Mariana.	Mariana **did not help** her mother.
I **lived** in Canada last year.	I **did not live** in San Antonio last year.
They **studied** on Saturday afternoon.	They **did not study** on Saturday night.

Contractions

did not = **didn't**

Rules for Simple Past Tense

If . . .	Then . . .	Example
If the verb ends in a consonant	then add **-ed**.	help → help**ed**
If the verb ends in **-e**	then add **-d**.	live → live**d**
If the verb ends in **consonant + y**	then change **y** to **i** and add **-ed**.	study → stud**ied**
If the verb ends in a vowel + consonant	then double the consonant and add **-ed**.	shop → shop**ped**

Used to (pg. 94)

Use **used to + the infinitive** to show that an activity was repeated or habitual in the past, but is no longer done.

Used to

Affirmative	Negative
My cousins **used to live** down the street.	My aunts **did not use to work** in offices.

Past Continuous Tense (pp. 33, 93)

Use the **past continuous tense** to talk about an action that was in progress at a specific time in the past.

Past Continuous Tense

Affirmative	Negative
I **was writing** a letter.	I **was not doing** homework.
Jennifer **was laughing**.	She **was not crying**.
They **were eating** a piece of cake.	They **were not eating** a slice of pie.

Irregular Verbs (p. 5, 78, 123)

Irregular verbs have special forms and are best memorized.

Past Tense of Irregular Verbs					
Base Form	Simple Past	Past participle	Base Form	Simple Past	Past participle
be	was/were	been	know	knew	known
become	became	become	leave	left	left
begin	began	begun	let	let	let
break	broke	broken	light	lit	lit
bring	brought	brought	lose	lost	lost
buy	bought	bought	make	made	made
catch	caught	caught	meet	met	met
choose	chose	chosen	pay	paid	paid
come	came	come	put	put	put
cost	cost	cost	read	read	read
cut	cut	cut	ride	rode	ridden
do	did	done	ring	rang	rang
drink	drank	drunk	run	ran	ran
drive	drove	driven	say	said	said
eat	ate	eaten	see	saw	seen
fall	fell	fallen	sell	sold	sold
feel	felt	felt	send	sent	sent
fight	fought	fought	sing	sang	sang
find	found	found	sit	sat	sat
fly	flew	flown	sleep	slept	slept
forget	forgot	forgotten	speak	spoke	spoken
get	got	gotten	spend	spent	spent
give	gave	given	stand	stood	stood
go	went	gone	take	took	taken
grow	grew	grown	teach	taught	taught
have	had	had	tell	told	told
hear	heard	heard	think	thought	thought
hold	held	held	wear	wore	worn
hurt	hurt	hurt	win	won	won
keep	kept	kept	write	wrote	written

FUTURE TENSE

The **future tense** describes events that happen after the present.

Simple Future Tense with *going to* (p. 5, 17)

Use the **simple future tense with *going to*** to express a definite plan. Use the **simple future tense with *going to*** or ***will*** to make predictions or talk about future plans.

Simple Future Tense with *going to*	
Affirmative	**Negative**
I **am going to go** shopping tonight.	I **am not going to go** shopping tomorrow.
You **are going to play** piano this afternoon.	You **are not going to play** volleyball.
The trip **is going to be** great.	The trip **is not going to be** boring.
We **are going to read** four books.	We **are not going to read** magazines.

Simple Future Tense with *will* (p. 17)

Use the **simple future tense with *will*** to make a promise.

Simple Future Tense with *will*	
Affirmative	**Negative**
I **will give** you my project tomorrow.	I **will not forget**.
We **will win** the game.	We **will not lose**.

Present Perfect (p. 78)

Use the **present perfect** to connect the past and the present. Use **have/has** + the **past participle** to make the **present perfect**. For most verbs, the past participle is the same as the simple past form. However, there are many verbs that have irregular past participles.

Present Perfect	
Affirmative	**Negative**
I **have enjoyed** working with children.	I **have not worked** with adults.
She **has visited** New York this year.	She **has not visited** Atlanta, Georgia.
We **have eaten** Chinese food before.	We **have not eaten** Thai food.

Use **for** and **since** with the present perfect. Use **for** + a period of time. Use **since** + a point in time.

I have lived here **for** two years.

She has lived here **since** June 1st.

Regular Verbs			Irregular Verbs		
Present	**Past**	**Past Participle**	**Present**	**Past**	**Past Participle**
fix	fixed	fixed	be	was/were	been
live	lived	lived	come	came	come
talk	talked	talked	drink	drank	drunk
walk	walked	walked	get	got	gotten

Passive Voice (p. 123)

Use the **passive voice** to focus on the result of an action, not the person who does the action.

Tense	The Passive Voice
Simple Present:	Candy **is (not) sold** at school. Our photos **are (not) found** on the Internet.
Simple Past:	The actor **was (not) admired** wherever he went. New software **was (not) developed** for this computer.

The subject of a passive verb corresponds to the object of an active verb.

Active Voice	Passive Voice
object Our school **performs** plays.	*subject* Plays **are performed** by our school.

Imperative Form (p. 47)

Use the **imperative form** to give instructions, directions, or orders. The imperative is like the simple present tense verb for **you** without the subject.

Simple Present	Imperative Sentences	
	Affirmative	**Negative**
You write a story.	**Write** a story.	**Do not write** a story.
You go to your piano class.	**Go** to your piano class.	**Do not go** to your piano class.

There was/were (p. 33)

There was/were		
	Affirmative	**Negative**
Singular	There **was** a piece of pie on the table.	There **was not** a piece of pie on the table.
Plural	There **were** many people at the cashier.	There **were not** many people at the cashier.
Noncount Nouns	There **was** ice cream in the freezer.	There **was not** any ice cream in the freezer.

Modal Verbs: *can, must, should* (p. 47)

Use a **modal verb** to help the verb give more information.

Modal Verbs		
Purpose	**Modal Verb**	
	Affirmative	**Negative**
ability	You **can** take the bus.	You **can not** take the train.
necessity	You **must** be careful when you cross the street.	You **must not** run.
recommendation	You **should** stay on Grand Street.	You **should not** go past the market.

Reported Speech (p. 65)

Use **reported speech** when you want to say what someone has said. Use *said* (that) + clause. In reported speech, the verb often changes to a different tense.

Direct speech shows exactly what the speaker said. It uses a comma and quotation marks.

Reported Speech	Direct Speech
She **said (that)** she **couldn't** go to the movies.	She said, "I **can't** go to the movies."
He **said (that)** he **didn't** trust me.	He said, "I **don't** trust you."

These words typically change tense in reported speech:

can → could

will → would

is going to → was going to

is studying → was studying

have to → had to

SENTENCES

Complete Sentences

A **sentence** is a group of words. The words express a complete thought.

A **complete sentence** has a subject and a verb.

The **subject** tells who or what the sentence is about.

The **verb** tells about the subject.

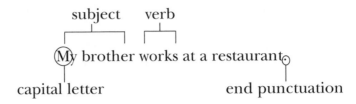

Incomplete Sentences (incorrect)	Complete Sentences (correct)
Carlos volleyball team. (no verb)	Carlos is on the volleyball team.
Writes in her journal. (no subject)	Hong writes in her journal.

Subject-Verb Agreement (p. 95)

The **subject** and **verb** in a sentence must **agree** in number.

When a subject is singular, the verb must be singular.

When a subject is plural, the verb must be plural.

Subject-Verb Agreement	
singular subject + singular verb	plural subject + plural verb
She is a doctor.	**They are** teachers.
The man cooks breakfast every day.	**The children play** in the park.

Compound Sentences (p. 18)

Use **compound sentences** to combine ideas from two shorter sentences that are equally important. Join the sentences with a connecting words like: **and, but, or, so, because**. Use a comma before the connecting word.

Example: Her eyes are dark brown. Her hair is wavy and black.

Her eyes are dark brown, **and** her hair is wavy and black.

She is funny. She is also very sensitive.

She is funny, **but** she is also very sensitive.

Compound Subjects and Predicates (pp. 18, 95, 137)

Use compound subjects to talk about two or more nouns in a sentence doing an action.

Example: John walked to school. Sarah walked to school.
John **and** Sarah walked to school.

Use compound verbs to talk about two or more actions in a sentence.

Example: Martin fumbled with the glass. Martin dropped the glass.
Martin fumbled with the glass **and** dropped it.

Complex Sentences (p. 63)

Use a complex sentence to combine two or more clauses (ideas). By joining the clauses (ideas) into a complex sentence, the sentence is clearer.

Independent clauses are complete sentences. Dependent clauses are not complete sentences. Join the clauses with words such as because and when. Use a comma after the dependent clause when it is at the beginning of the sentence.

Complex Sentences		
Dependent Clause	**Independent Clause**	**Sentence**
Because she was tired, . . .	She fell asleep on the couch.	Because she was tired, she fell asleep on the couch.
When they heard the noise, . . .	They turned around and saw the truck.	When they heard the noise, they turned around and saw the truck.

Complex Sentences with *if* Clauses (p. 107)

Use *if* clauses in future conditionals to talk about something that you think will happen in that situation. Use *will* in the independent clause.

Complex Sentences with if Clauses	
Dependent Clause (Condition)	**Independent Clause (Result)**
If I win the contest,	I will be happy.
If endangered animals lose their habitat,	they will die out.

If the *if* clause comes at the beginning of the sentence, place a comma after the *if* clause.

Example: *If* it rains tomorrow, I will stay home.

If the *if* clause comes at the end of the sentence, do not use a comma.

Example: I will stay home *if* it rains tomorrow.

Indirect Requests (p. 77)

Use **indirect request** to ask for something in a formal or polite manner. It is often used in formal letters.

Indirect Requests	Direct Requests
Would you **please** send me information?	**Please** send me information.
Would you **please** give me the instructions?	**Please** give me the instructions.

Parallel Structures (p. 123)

Use **parallel structures** to join two or more nouns or **noun phrases** or verbs or verb **phrases** in a sentence.

A **verb phrase** is a verb joined with another word or words in a sentence. If a sentence has more than one **verb phrase**, the verbs must all agree or have the same form.

A **noun phrase** is a noun joined with another word or words in a sentence. If a sentence has more than one **noun phrase** together, the nouns must all agree or be the same form.

Parallel Structures	
Verb Phrase Agreement	**Noun Phrase Agreement**
She **worked** hard and **finished** her project.	Pets need **lots of food** and **lots of exercise**.
The leader **lead** the projects, **kept** us focused, and **worked** hard.	I admire her for her **work, dedication, and success**.

Relative Clauses with *who* and *that* (p. 107)

Relative clauses tell more about a noun in a sentence. If a relative clause describes a person, *who* or *that* starts the clause.

Example: The teacher loves the student **who** hands in homework.
The teacher loves the student **that** hands in homework.

If a **relative clause** describes an animal or a thing, *that* starts the clause.

Example: The veterinarian loves the dog **that** doesn't bite.

ADJECTIVES

Adjectives (pp. 5, 16, 32, 62, 76, 92, 106, 122, 136)

Adjectives describe or give information about people, places, or things.

Adjectives go after the verb or before a noun. Add a comma (,) or the word **and** between adjectives.

Her hair is **wavy**.	Her face is **long** and **thin**.
He is a **good** student.	They are **serious, honest** people.

Possessive Adjectives

Possessive adjectives tell who owns something. Place the possessive adjective before a noun.

Possessive Adjective	Examples
my	I am a student. **My** name is Rafael.
your	You are a freshman. **Your** homeroom is Room 21.
his	Sam is a student. **His** teacher is Mr. Li.
her	This is Julia. This is **her** classroom.
its	The computer is in the office. **Its** screen is on.
our	We are studying biology. **Our** teacher is Mrs. Johnson.
your	You are good students. **Your** grades are excellent.
their	Mr. and Mrs. Garcia are parents. **Their** son is Francisco.

Comparative and Superlative Adjectives

Comparative adjectives compare two things.

Add than after the comparative form.

> Maria is **younger than** John.
>
> Maria's costume is **more interesting than** Tara's costume.

Forms of Comparative Adjectives

If . . .	Then . . .	Example
If the adjective has one syllable	then add **er**.	small → small**er**
If the adjective has two syllables and ends in **y**	then change the **y** to **i** and add **er**.	happy → happ**ier**
If the adjective ends in **e**	then add **r**.	nice → nice**r**
If the adjective has two or more syllables	then add **more** before the adjective.	interesting → **more** interesting
If the adjective is irregular	then use the comparative adjective form.	good → **better** bad → **worse**

Superlative adjectives compare more than two things.

Add the before the superlative form.

> Maria is **the youngest** person in her family.
>
> Maria's costume is **the most interesting** in her class.

Forms of Superlative Adjectives

If . . .	Then . . .	Example
The adjective has one syllable	then add **est**.	small → small**est**
The adjective has two syllables and ends in **y**	then change the **y** to **i** and add **est**.	happy → happ**iest**
The adjective ends in **e**	then add **st**.	nice → nice**st**
The adjective has two or more syllables	then add **most** before the adjective.	interesting → **most** interesting
The adjective is irregular	then use the superlative adjective form.	good → **best** bad → **worst**

Adjective Formation (p. 139)

The base word form of a word can be turned into an adjective by adding the ending
-y, -ing, -ed.

Adjective Formation	
Base word	**Ending**
hunger	hung**ry**
exaggerate	exaggerat**ing**
scare	scar**ed**

L. A. T. C. Mission College
3000 Mission College Blvd.
Santa Clara, CA 95054
(408) 855-5095

Predicate Adjectives (p. 16)

Predicate adjectives follow linking verbs like the verb **to be**. They are placed after the verb.

Predicate Adjective	Sentence
black and wavy	Her hair **is black and wavy**.
kind	They **are kind**.

Quantity Adjectives (p. 34)

Quantity adjectives answer the question how much or how many.

Quantity Adjectives	
Large Amounts	**Small amounts**
All of my friends are in China.	I had **some** bad luck.
A lot of buses were driving down the street.	There are **a few** people outside.
There were **many** people at the park.	**One of** the cars splashed me.

Adjective Phrases (p. 34, 138)

Adjective phrases are a group of words that describe a noun.

Adjective Phrases		
Noun	**Adjective Phrase**	**Sentence**
story	few weaknesses	The **story** has **few weaknesses**.
author	out-of-place words	The **author** uses **out-of-place words**.

ADVERBS

Adverbs (pp. 6, 16)

Adverbs answer the questions *how, when,* or *where.* They give details about verbs, adjectives, and other adverbs. To make many adverbs, add **-ly** to the adjective form. *Really, yesterday,* and *very* are also adverbs.

Adverbs	
Use	**Purpose**
She watches them **carefully**.	The adverb tells **how** she watches them.
It is **really** hot.	The adverb tells **how** hot it is.
Yesterday, I ran in the park.	The adverb tells **when** I ran.
There is a store **nearby**.	The adverb tells **where** the store is.

Many adverbs are made of an adjective **+ly**.

Adjective	+ -ly	Adverb
Quick	add **-ly**	quick**ly**
happy	change **y** to **i**, add **-ly**	happ**ily**
simple	drop e, add **-ly**	simp**ly**

Adverbs of Frequency (p. 6)

Adverbs of frequency answer the question how often.

Adverbs of Frequency		
How often?	**Adverb of Frequency**	**Example**
100% of the time	always	I walk to school every day. I **always** walk to school.
	usually	I bring my lunch four days per week. I **usually** bring my lunch.
	often	I arrive early three days per week. I **often** arrive early.
	sometimes	I am very tired one or two days per week. I am **sometimes** very tired.
0% of the time	never	I don't dance. I **never** dance.

PREPOSITIONS

Prepositions (pp. 5, 35)

Prepositions tell where, when, and how something happens. They usually have a noun after them.

Prepositional phrases are made up of:

preposition + noun = **prepositional phrase**

to   a restaurant
through   a puddle of water
at   home

Common Prepositions				
about	before	by	in	through
above	behind	during	into	to
across	below	except	of	under
around	beside	for	on	with
at	between	from	over	without

Prepositions of Time (p. 5)

Time phrases tell when something happens or how long something lasts.

Example: I play basketball **for** two hours **on** the weekend.

When?	**in** the morning	**on** Saturday	**at** 12:00 P.M./**at** noon
How long?	**for** two hours	**for** two weeks	**from** 3:00 **to** 5:00

Prepositions of Location

Location Phrases tell where something is located.

Where?	**on** Elm Street	**at** Oak Street Park	**across from** Room 21

DO NOT WRITE IN THIS BOOK

Conjunctions

Conjunctions connect parts of a sentence. They can join words and phrases. They can also join two clauses.

Coordinating conjunctions can join more than one subject, verb, or independent clause (a clause that can stand alone). When there are more than three words or word groups, use a coordinating conjunction to join the last two.

*Lisa researched the topic, took notes, **and** wrote the report.*

Coordinating Conjunctions		
and	for	so
but	or	yet

Subordinating conjunctions connect an independent clause (a clause that stands alone) with a dependent clause (a clause that cannot stand alone).

Independent clause   dependent clause

I washed the dishes   *before I went to the game.*

Subordinating Conjunctions		
Conjunction	**Use**	**Example**
When before after	Tells when something happened	I finished my project **before** I went to the game. **Before** I went to the game, I finished my project
because	Gives a reason	She researched the country **because** she was interested. **Because** she was interested, she researched the country.
although	Shows a contrast	They walked home **although** it was late. **Although** it was late, they walked home.

PUNCTUATION

Period (.)
end of a statement	I go to school.
after an abbreviation	Ave. Mr. St. Dr.

Question Mark (?)
end of a question	How are you?

Exclamation Point (!)
after a strong sentence	My room is very small!

Apostrophe (')
to show possession	The girl's book is on the desk.
in a contraction	he's it's isn't weren't didn't

Comma (,)
to separate things in a list	Victoria, Yang, and I are classmates.
to separate adjectives	The short, funny man is in the park.
between the day and year in a date	July 4, 1776
between city and state	Dallas, Texas
after the opening of a friendly letter	Dear Roxana,
after the closing of a letter	Sincerely,

CAPITALIZATION

Capitalize the first word in a sentence.	He is from Los Angeles.
Capitalize the pronoun **I**.	Jose and **I** are best friends.
Capitalize proper nouns.	
people	George Washington
places	Puebla, Mexico
days	Monday
months	February
holidays	Thanksgiving
special events	Olympics
nationalities	British
languages	Spanish
schools	West High School
abbreviations	Dr. Rd.
titles	*Step-by-Step Writing*

English spelling has some general rules. If you are not sure of how to spell a word, check it in a dictionary.

General Rules	Example
ie* and *ei • Use *i* before *e* except after *c*. • Use *i* before *e* except when letters are pronounced *ay* as in *eight*.	***i* before *e***: *piece* *friend* ***ei* after *c***: *receive* *ceiling* ***ei* pronounced *ay***: *weigh* *neighbor*
q* and *u • Place the letter *u* after the letter *q*.	Do you have any **qu**estions before the *qui*z?
Plurals • Add *-es* to words that end in *s, ss, sh, ch, x,* and *z*. • If a word ends in a consonant plus *y*, change the *y* to *i* and add *–es*. • For all other words, add *–s*.	They set the *dishes* on the table. The *ladies* sat and talked. She collects *stamps*.
Doubling Final Consonants • When you add an ending to one-syllable words with one vowel that end in a consonant, double the last consonant.	The boy dro**pp**ed the toy on the floor. The green box was the *biggest* of the two.
Silent *e* Before a Suffix • Keep the silent *e* when a suffix beginning with a consonant is added to a word, for example, *-ful, -ness,* or *–ment*. • Drop the silent *e* when a suffix beginning with a vowel is added to a word, for example, *-ed, -es, -ing, -er,* or *-est*.	The team was *hopeful* they win. The concert was very liv**ely**. They *hoped* the test was not difficult. I am *having* some cake. Would you like some?

COMMONLY MISSPELLED WORDS

Word	Definition	Sentence
allowed aloud	permitted; with permission out loud, spoken	Being late is not **allowed.** The student read her poem **aloud** in class.
among between	included within in the space separating two things	**Among** her many friends, she is happy. The cat was **between** the wall and the car.
board bored	a classroom object for writing on tired, uninterested	Please write the answer on the **board.** The class is not interesting, so I am **bored.**
buy by	to pay for something next to	I **buy** a newspaper every morning. The chair is **by** the door.
cite sight site	to give credit to a source of information the sense of seeing a real location or one on Internet	In his report, the student **cites** several books. My **sight** is good. I don't need glasses. The information is on our Web **site.**
desert dessert	dry land of sand and rock, with little rain food after a meal, like cake or fruit	The Sahara **Desert** is in Africa. We had apple pie and coffee for **dessert.**
for four	with the purpose of the number 4	I am buying tomatoes **for** the salad. The boy has **four** sisters.
hear here	to receive sound with the ears at or in this place	I **hear** the sound of a police car. We have lived **here** for ten years.
it's its	a contraction of *it is* the possessive form of *it*	**It's** raining today, but it wasn't yesterday. The house has a tree by **its** door.
than then	used to show comparison the next in an order of events	The weather is hotter **than** it was last year. I went to school and **then** I went to work.
their there they're	the possessive form of *they* at or to a specific place used to begin a statement a contraction of *they are*	**Their** apartment is on the second floor. We went **there** after school. **There** are twenty students in class today. **They're** tired because they ran home.
to too two	toward, in the direction of in addition, as well, also the number 2	She goes **to** Vietnam every year. The book was good. The movie was good **too.** People have **two** legs.
we're were where	a contraction of *we are* past tense of *be* in or at which place, a certain location	**We're** having dinner after work. They **were** at the store this morning. **Where** are you from?
who's whose	a contraction of *who is* the possessive form of *who*	**Who's** going to come to our party? **Whose** coat is this?
your you're	the possessive form of *you* a contraction of *you are*	Is this **your** hat? **You're** sick. You should stay home.

Paragraph Model

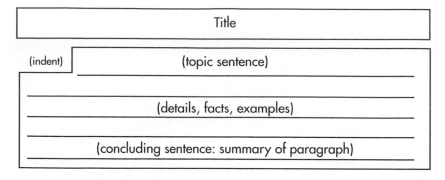

Friendly Letter Model   ## Formal Letter Model

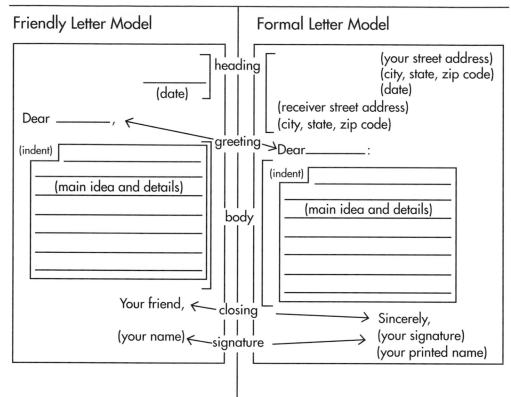

CITATION GUIDE

Book with One Author

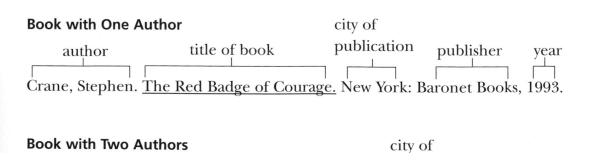

author | title of book | city of publication | publisher | year

Crane, Stephen. <u>The Red Badge of Courage.</u> New York: Baronet Books, 1993.

Book with Two Authors

authors | title of book | city of publication | publisher | year

Berkow, Loren, and Barry Smith. <u>Carrying the World</u>. Boston: Goalpost Publishing, 2004.

Magazine

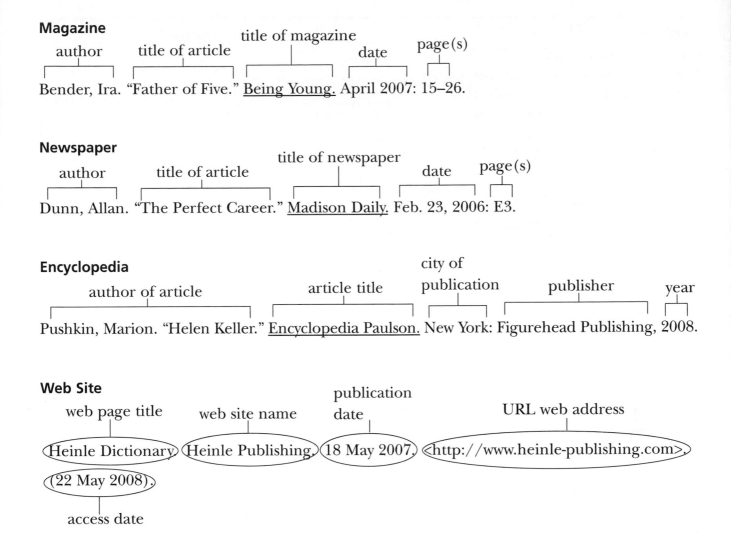

author   title of article   title of magazine   date   page(s)

Bender, Ira. "Father of Five." Being Young. April 2007: 15–26.

Newspaper

author   title of article   title of newspaper   date   page(s)

Dunn, Allan. "The Perfect Career." Madison Daily. Feb. 23, 2006: E3.

Encyclopedia

author of article   article title   city of publication   publisher   year

Pushkin, Marion. "Helen Keller." Encyclopedia Paulson. New York: Figurehead Publishing, 2008.

Web Site

web page title   web site name   publication date   URL web address

Heinle Dictionary. Heinle Publishing. 18 May 2007. <http://www.heinle-publishing.com>.

(22 May 2008).

access date

STUDENT WRITING RUBRIC

Look at the writing. Read the sentences below. Add your own criteria at the end of the list. Do you agree with the sentences? Look at the score chart. Then, write a score next to each sentence. Add comments.

Score		Meaning
5		I strongly agree.
4		I agree.
3		I have no opinion.
2		I disagree.
1		I strongly disagree.

Criteria	Score	Comments
1. Development of Ideas		
The author answered the prompt completely.		
The writing has a purpose or main idea.		
All the ideas connect to a main idea.		
The details support the main ideas.		
The author shows an understanding of the topic.		
2. Organization		
The writing has an introduction, a body, and a conclusion.		
The ideas are in a logical order.		
The paragraphs are well-organized.		
3. Voice		
The author's voice is original.		
The writing is interesting.		
The writing addresses the correct audience.		
4. Fluency and Focus		
The writing maintains focus.		
There are meaningful transitions between ideas.		
The sentences and paragraphs are clear and concise.		
There are different sentence types.		
5. Conventions		
The sentences use correct grammar.		
The words and phrases are specific and meaningful.		
The punctuation and capitalization are correct.		
The spelling is correct.		
The author cites sources correctly.		
6. Presentation		
The presentation is in the correct format.		
The author included a title, name, and date.		
The first line of every paragraph is indented.		
7. My Criteria		
-		
-		
Total		
÷ 25		
Grade (out of 5)		

What your grade means:

5	4	3	2	1
excellent	great	good	need more practice	incomplete

active voice, p. 123 The **active voice** is used to focus on the person who is doing the action.

adjectives, p. 16 **Adjectives** describe or give information about nouns.

adjective phrases, p. 138 **Adjective phrases** are phrases that describe nouns.

adverbs of frequency, p. 6 **Adverbs of frequency** describe how often an event occurs.

antonyms, p. 16 An **antonym** is a word that has an opposite meaning to another word.

beginning, p. 65, 66 The **beginning** of a story introduces the story and tells about the setting and the characters.

bibliography, p. 125 A **bibliography** is a list of sources that you used to research the information you included in your report.

biographical description, p. 20 A **biographical description** can describe how a person looks, acts, what they like, and what they mean to the writer.

biographies, p. 124, 128 **Biographies** are true stories about someone's life, written by another person. Biographies include important dates, events, and people in the person's life.

body paragraph, p. 108 A **body paragraph** explains and gives the thesis in a research report.

cause, p. 64 A **cause** is the reason why an event or situation occurs.

cause-and-effect words, p. 64 **Cause-and-effect words** signal one event is the result of another. Examples: *as a result, therefore, because, then.*

characters, p. 65, 66 **Characters** are the people in a story.

chronological order, p. 5, 124 **Chronological order** is the order in which events really happen in a story.

clause, p. 63 A **clause** is a group of words with a subject and a verb.

closing, p. 35, 79 In the **closing,** the sender of a letter says "good bye" to the receiver of the letter.

colon, p. 79 A **colon** is a punctuation mark used to start a list. It follows a complete sentence.

comma, p. 7, 65 A **comma** is a punctuation mark that can be used in many ways, but is mainly used for separating things.

compare and contrast essays, p. 94, 96 In a **compare and contrast essay** the thesis statement tells what two things are being compared and contrasted.

compare and contrast signal words, p. 95 **Compare and contrast signal words** show that two topics are being compared or contrasted.

compare, p. 94 To **compare** two things means to assess their similarities.

complex sentences, p. 63, 107 **Complex sentences** include both an independent and dependent clause.

complex sentences with *if* clauses, p. 107 **Complex sentences with if clauses** express a possible situation that you think will happen. The *if clause* may come at the beginning or end of a sentence.

compound predicate, p. 137 **Compound predicates** occur in a sentence when more than one separate verb or verb phrase is being performed in the sentence.

compound sentences, p. 19 **Compound sentences** are two or more complete sentences combined with a connecting word.

compound, p. 137 A **Compound** means more than one. p. 19, 137 **Compound subjects** occur when two or more nouns perform the action in a sentence.

compound verbs, p. 19 **Compound verbs** are two or more verbs in a sentence.

concluding sentence, p. 8, 18 The **concluding sentence** ends the story and tells what it means.

connecting word, p. 19 A **connecting word,** like *or, but, and* or *because,* joins ideas or sentences.

continuous tenses, p. 33 **Continuous tenses** include the present continuous tense and the past continuous tense.

contractions, p. 17, 33 A **contraction,** like *he's* and *can't,* is one word made from two words put together with an apostrophe.

contrast, p. 94 To **contrast** two things means to assess their differences.

dates, events, and people, p. 126 Important **dates, events, and people** are usually included in biographies.

day and time phrases, p. 5 **Day and time phrases** are used to describe when events took place.

dependent clause, p. 63, 107 A **dependent clause** is in a complex sentence and cannot be a complete sentence by itself.

descriptive writing, p. 20 **Descriptive writing** gives details and information about a topic.

details, p. 7, 18 **Details** give more information about a main idea.

direct request, p. 77 **Direct requests** use *please* and the infinitive to ask a polite request.

direct speech, p. 65 **Direct speech** gives the actual words that a person said.

effect, p. 64 An **effect** is the result or outcome of a situation.

e-mail, p. 36 An **e-mail** is an electronic message sent using the Internet.

end, p. 65, 66 The **end** of a story tells what the story means or why it is important.

evidence, p. 109 **Evidence** is information that proves something is true.

example phrases, p. 109 **Example phrases** are used to tell that evidence is being given.

express your opinion, p. 139 When you **express your opinion,** you say what you think or feel about a subject.

facts, p. 109 **Facts** are true statements about a subject.

formal letter, p. 79, 80 A **formal letter** gives more background information and uses more formal language than friendly letters. A formal letter is usually used when a writer is writing to someone they don't know. Business letters and event invitations are examples of formal letters.

friendly letter, p. 35, 36 A **friendly letter** is an informal letter that is written to a friend or family member.

greeting, p. 35, 79 In the **greeting** of a letter, the writer says "hello" to the receiver.

homonyms, p. 49 **Homonyms** are words that sound the same but have different meanings and spellings.

hyperlink, p. 12, 42, 72, 86, 102 A **hyperlink** is something you can click on a Web page, opening a new Web site.

imperative sentences, p. 47 **Imperative sentences** are commands that are used to tell people what to do.

in agreement, p. 95 Verbs must always be **in agreement** with their nouns, meaning that singular nouns are followed by the singular form of the verb and plural nouns are followed by the plural form of the verb.

indented, p. 7 When you **indent,** you leave space before writing a line of text.

independent clause, p. 63, 107 An **independent clause** is part of a complex sentence that is a complete sentence.

indirect requests, p. 77 **Indirect requests** use *Would like to* make requests.

informal message, p. 36 An **informal message,** like a friendly letter or an e-mail, is usually written to a friend or family member. It often tells how the author is feeling and about recent events or activities.

keyword search, p. 12, 26, 42, 50, 72, 86, 102, 116, 126 A **keyword search** is a search that uses a specific word or words to look up information on the Internet.

linking verbs, p. 16 **Linking verbs** connect the subject and predicate of a clause.

literature reviews, p. 140 Literature reviews tell about books or stories and give general information about the setting, characters, and plot as well as discussing the strengths and weaknesses and giving examples for each one.

main idea, p. 7 The **main idea** (or controlling idea) is the focus, central thought, or purpose of a paragraph.

main supporting sentences, p. 18 Main supporting sentences give details, or more information, about the topic sentence.

middle, p. 65, 66 The **middle** of a story gives details about the action or plot.

minor supporting sentences, p. 18 Minor supporting sentences add more information about each main supporting sentence.

modal verbs, p. 47 Modal verbs are helping verbs that give more information.

narration, p. 8 Narration tells a story.

noun phrase, p. 123 A **noun phrase** is a noun joined with another word or words in a sentence. If a sentence has more than one noun phrase together, the nouns must all agree or be in the same form.

nouns, p. 49, 95 A **noun** is any word that is a person, place, or a thing.

order of importance, p. 79 Order of importance tells the most important point first, the second point next, and the least important point last.

organizers, p. 124 Organizers are tools to help you organize ideas for your writing. Examples: outlines, web, two-column chart.

outlines, p. 124 Outlines are a graphic organizer used to plan and organize ideas. Main ideas are numbered and supporting evidence and ideas are lettered.

paragraph, p. 7 A **paragraph** is a group of sentences about a topic.

parallel structure, p. 123 A sentence has a **parallel structure** when the words, phrases, or clauses of a sentence use the same tense or similar language.

paraphrase, p. 109 To **paraphrase** is to retell in a writer's own words information from a source.

past continuous tense, p. 33, 93 The **past continuous tense** is used to describe an event that started in the past, continued for a while in the past, and ended in the past.

passive voice, p. 123 The **passive voice** is used to focus on the receiver or the result of the action.

past tense with used to, p. 94 The **past tense with used to** with the infinitive of a verb talk about habits or routines that happened frequently in the past but that are no longer.

plot, p. 65 The **plot** is the series of main events that make up a story.

predicate adjectives, p. 16 Predicate adjectives are adjectives that follow linking verbs and are used differently than adjectives placed before the noun.

preposition, p. 5, 34 A **preposition** is a short connecting word, such as *to, from, with,* and *in,* that shows how two things or ideas are related.

present continuous tense, p. 33 The **present continuous tense** describes an event that is happening in the present.

present perfect tense, p. 78 The **present perfect tense** is used to express an activity that started in the past and continues until the present. It is formed but using has/have and the past participle of a verb.

pronouns, p. 49, 64 Pronouns take the place of nouns and refer back to the words they replace. Examples: *he, she, it, they, we us.*

quantity adjectives, p. 34 Quantity adjectives are adjectives that tell the amount, or how many, of a noun there is. Example: *Many* books; *some* students.

quotation marks, p. 65 Quotation marks are a type of punctuation used at the beginning and end of a quote, or the actual words a person has said.

quote, p. 109 A **Quote** is what a source says exactly.

receiver, p. 36 The **receiver** is the person who a letter is written for.

relative clauses, p. 107 **Relative clauses** tell more about a noun in a sentence.

relative clauses with *who* and *that*, p. 107 When a **relative clause** describes a person, *who* starts the clause. When the clause describes an animal or a thing, *that* starts the clause.

reported speech, p. 65 **Reported speech** tells what someone said and does not use quotes.

research reports, p. 108, 110 **Research reports** are organized essays that give facts and information about a topic.

resumé, p. 78 A **resumé** is a list and description of someone's work and education experiences.

search, p. 12 To **search** is to look up information on the Internet.

sender, p. 79 The **sender** is the person who writes a letter.

sensory adjectives, p. 32 **Sensory adjectives** describe how things smell, feel, taste, sound, and look.

sequence of events, p. 124 The **sequence of events** refers to the order that things happen in a story. In a biography, the **sequence of events** are usually in chronological order.

sequence words, p. 7, 48 **Sequence words** are used to show the order of events.

sequential order, p. 48 **Sequential order** tells the order of events.

setting, p. 66 **Setting** is the time and place of the story.

signal words, p. 19 **Signal words**, like *too* and *as well,* add information in a story.

simple future tense with *be going to*, p. 17 The **simple future tense with be going to** is used to express a definite plan that will happen later, or in the future.

simple future tense with *will*, p. 17 The **simple future tense with will** is used to express a promise.

simple past tense, p. 93 The **simple past** is used to talk about something that started and ended in the past and is formed by adding –*ed*. Some irregular verbs need the stem changed before adding –*ed*.

simple verb tense, p. 5 A **simple verb tense** is a verb with no endings or other changes. For example, *walk, speak,* and *see* are in the simple verb tense.

spatial descriptions, p. 34 **Spatial descriptions** use prepositions to describe where something is located or where an action takes place.

spatial order, p. 35 **Spatial order** can be used to describe a place; it gives information by location or the way the writer sees places.

story, p. 65, 66 A **Story** is a piece of writing that is made up in the writer's mind.

strengths, p. 138 **Strengths** are positive qualities.

subject, p. 64 The **subject** tells who or what the sentence is about.

summarize, p. 109 To **summarize** means to create a shortened or simplified version of the original.

supporting sentences, p. 7, 8 A **supporting sentence** gives details or more information about the topic.

synonyms, p. 16 A **Synonym** is a word that has the same or similar meaning to another word.

technical writing, p. 50 **Technical writing** often gives instructions. It sometimes explains how to do a procedure.

thesis statement, p. 94, 108 A **thesis statement** is a sentence at the end of the introduction paragraph that tells the main points of an essay.

timelines, p. 124 A **timeline** organizes events by time.

times and days, p. 6 **Times** and **days** are examples of words used to show chronological order.

topic, p. 7 A **topic** is what the paragraph or story is about.

topic sentence, p. 7, 8, 18, 94 A **topic sentence** is the sentence that gives the main idea of the paragraph.

verb phrase, p. 123 A **verb phrase** is a verb joined with another word or words in a sentence. If a sentence has more than one verb phrase together, the verbs must all agree or be in the same form.

verbs, p. 95 A **verb** is any word that tells the action of the subject.

weaknesses, p. 138 **Weaknesses** are negative qualities.

INDEX

Technology

Vocabulary and Language

Writing

Writing Conventions and Strategies